Measurement Uncertainty Methods and Applications

An Independent Learning Module
from the
Instrument Society of America

MEASUREMENT UNCERTAINTY METHODS AND APPLICATIONS

By Ronald H. Dieck

 INSTRUMENT SOCIETY OF AMERICA

Copyright © 1992 Instrument Society of America

Printed in the United States of America

INSTRUMENT SOCIETY OF AMERICA
67 Alexander Drive
P.O. Box 12277
Research Triangle Park
North Carolina 27709

Library of Congress Cataloging-in-Publication Data
Dieck, Ronald H.
  Measurement uncertainty: methods and applications / by Ronald H.
Dieck.
    p.   cm. — (An Independent learning module from the Instrument
Society of America)
  Includes bibliographical references and index.
  ISBN 1-55617-126-9
  1. Mensuration. 2. Uncertainty. I. Title. II. Series.
T50.D53   1992   92-24674
620'.0044—dc20   CIP

Second printing January 1995

TABLE OF CONTENTS

PREFACE

This book is an Independent Learning Module (ILM) as developed and published by the Instrument Society of America (ISA). The ILMs are the principal components of a major education system designed primarily for independent self-study. This comprehensive learning system has been custom designed and created for ISA to more fully educate people in the basic theories and technologies associated with applied instrumentation and control.

The ILM System is divided into several distinct sets of Modules on closely related topics; such a set of individually related Modules is called a Series. The ILM System is composed of:

- the ISA Series of Modules on Control Principles and Techniques;
- the ISA Series of Modules on Fundamental Instrumentation;
- the ISA Series of Modules on Unit Process and Unit Operation Control;
- the ISA Series of Modules for Professional Development;
- the ISA Series of Modules on Specific Industries; and
- the ISA Series of Modules on Software-Assisted Topics.

The principal components of the series are the individual ILMs (or Modules) such as this one. They are especially designed for independent self-study; no other text or references are required. The unique format, style, and teaching techniques employed in the ILMs make them a powerful addition to any library.

The published ILMs are as follows:

Fundamentals of Process Control Theory—Paul W. Murrill—1981

Controlling Multivariable Processes—F. G. Shinskey—1981

Microprocessors in Industrial Control—Robert J. Bibbero—1982

Measurement and Control of Liquid Level—Chun H. Cho—1982

Control Valve Selection and Sizing—Les Dreskell—1983

Fundamentals of Flow Measurement—Joseph P. DeCarlo—1984

Intrinsic Safety—E. C. Magison—1984

Digital Control—Theodore J. Williams—1984

pH Control—Gregory K. McMillan—1985

FORTRAN Programming—James M. Pruett—1986

Introduction to Telemetry—O. J. Strock—1987

Application Concepts in Process Control—Paul W. Murrill—1988

Controlling Centrifugal Compressors—Ralph L. Moore—1989

CIM in the Process Industries—John W. Bernard—1989

Continuous Control Techniques for Distributive Control Systems—Gregory K. McMillan—1989

Temperature Measurement in Industry—E. C. Magison—1990

Simulating Process Control Loops Using BASIC—F. G. Shinskey—1990

Tuning of Industrial Control Systems—Armando B. Corripio—1990

Computer Control Strategies—Albert A. Gunkler and John W. Bernard—1990

Environmental Control Systems—Randy D. Down—1992

Auditing and Justification of Control Systems—N. E. (Bill) Battikha—1992

Measurement Uncertainty Methods and Applications—Ronald H. Dieck—1992

Most of the original ILMs were envisioned to be the more traditional or fundamental subjects in instrumentation and process control. With the publications planned over the next few years, the ILM Series will become much more involved in emerging technologies.

ISA has increased its commitment to the ILM Series and has set for itself a goal of publishing four ILMs each year. Obviously, this growing Series is part of a foundation for any professional library in instrumentation and control. The individual practitioner will find them of value, of course, and they are a necessity in any institutional or corporate library.

There is obvious value in maintaining continuity within your personal set of ILMs; place a standing purchase order with ISA.

Paul W. Murrill
Consulting Editor, ILM Series
May, 1992

Comments about This Volume

This ILM, *Measurement Uncertainty Methods and Applications*, is designed to provide an understanding of the importance of the role of measurement uncertainty analysis in any test or experimental measurement process. No test data should be considered without a knowledge of its uncertainty. Many examples are included to illustrate the principles and applications of measurement uncertainty analysis.

This material will be useful to test engineers, process engineers, control engineers, researchers, plant supervisors, managers, executives, and all others who need a basic understanding of the assessment and impact of uncertainty in test and experimental measurements. In addition, technical school, college, and university students will find this course useful in gaining insight into the impact of errors in their measurements as well as in estimating the effects of these errors with measurement uncertainty analysis.

Acknowledgments

The author wishes to acknowledge the assistance of Mike Englund, Gil Moore, and Barbara Ringhiser, whose willing and thorough review of this manuscript led to a more complete, correct, and comprehensible text. Thanks also go to my editor, Dr. Paul Murrill, who guided the creation of this ILM. Special appreciation is noted as well for the original and pioneering work of Dr. Robert Abernethy, whose early studies permitted the development of the universal uncertainty model, which is fundamental to the methods of this text. And finally, my personal and most sincere gratitude goes to my Lord and Savior Jesus Christ, who saw fit to grant me the talents and abilities without which this writing would not have been possible at all. In Him there is no uncertainty, only the certainty of life everlasting.

Ron Dieck, 1992

Dedication

The author wishes to dedicate this ILM to his wife, Donna, and to his three children, Mark, Duane, and Heidi.

Unit 1:
Introduction and Overview

UNIT 1

Introduction and Overview

Welcome to ISA's Independent Learning Module *Measurement Uncertainty Methods and Applications*. The first unit of this self-study program provides the information needed to proceed through the course.

Learning Objectives — When you have completed this unit, you should:

    A. Know the nature of material to be presented.

    B. Understand the general organization of the course.

    C. Know the course objectives.

1-1. Course Coverage

This course includes the basics of the measurement uncertainty model, the use of correlation, curve fitting problems, probability plotting, combining results from different test methods, calibration errors, and error propagation for both independent and dependent error sources. Extra attention is placed on the problem of developing confidence in uncertainty analysis results and on using measurement uncertainty to select instrumentation systems. Special emphasis on understanding is achieved through the working of numerous exercises. After completing this course, the student will be able to apply uncertainty analysis techniques to most experimental test problems in order to help achieve the test objectives more productively and at lower cost.

1-2. Purpose

The purpose of this ILM is to convey to the student a comprehensive knowledge of measurement uncertainty methods through documentation that is logically categorized and readily utilized in practical situations that confront an experimenter. Course structure is purposely divided into units that represent specific segments of measurement uncertainty methodology. Using this approach, the student will be able to proceed through the text, learn the methodology in an orderly fashion, and then return to specific topics as the need arises during experimental analysis.

The ILM contains numerous exercises intended to provide practical experience in working measurement uncertainty problems; several example calculations are presented to provide learning clarity for specific principles.

1-3. Audience and Prerequisites

This course is intended for scientists and engineers who are interested in evaluating experimental measurement uncertainty.

The course is presented on the college level and presumes that the student has received two years' training in engineering or science, can handle rudimentary principles of calculus, and has a calculator to work the examples and exercises.

The material should be useful to test engineers, senior technicians, first- and second-line supervisors, and engineers/ scientists who are concerned with deriving meaningful conclusions from experimental data. It should also be useful to students in technical schools, colleges, and universities who wish to gain some insight into the principles and practices of measurement uncertainty.

1-4. Study Material

This textbook is the only study material required in this course. It is one of ISA's several Independent Learning Modules on fundamental instrumentation and is designed as an independent, stand-alone textbook. It is uniquely and specifically structured for self-study. A list of suggested readings (Appendix A) provides additional references and study materials.

1-5. Organization and Sequence

This ILM is divided into seven separate units. Unit 2 is designed to provide the student an introduction to the conceptual thinking and basic statistics required for measurement uncertainty analysis. Unit 3 provides the details of a measurement uncertainty statement, including the proper characterization of error sources and their combination into an uncertainty statement for a test result. Unit 4 outlines a step-by-step method for summarizing the effects of various error sources and their treatment both before a test and after a test is run. Unit 5 deals with several specific methods required for knowledgeable uncertainty analysis. Special attention is paid to error propagation, the determination of the effect of an error source on a test result, and weighing results by their uncertainty, which is a method for obtaining a test result more accurate than any of several independent measurements of the same result. Unit 6 contains several practical application techniques for dealing with error data. These techniques are often needed during the course of computing measurement uncertainty. The book culminates with Unit 7, which contains a comprehensive treatment on the presentation of measurement uncertainty analysis results.

Each unit is designed in a consistent format with a set of specific learning objectives stated in the very beginning of the unit. Note these learning objectives carefully; the material that follows the learning objectives will teach to these objectives. The individual units often contain example problems to illustrate specific concepts. At the end of each unit, you will find student exercises to test your understanding of the material. The solutions to all exercises may be found in Appendix I.

1-6. Course Objectives/Learning Objectives

When you have completed this entire Independent Learning Module, you should be able to:

A. Describe the basic approach to evaluating measurement uncertainty.

B. Converse comfortably using measurement uncertainty and fundamental statistical terminology.

C. Complete a detailed measurement uncertainty analysis for any test or experiment, including defining the experimental setup, locating and estimating the magnitude of the random and systematic sources of error, propagating those errors into the test result, calculating the test result measurement uncertainty, and presenting the uncertainty analysis in a compelling fashion.

D. Explain the significance of a test's measurement uncertainty in order to better plan experiments and tests in a more cost-effective manner to yield test data more suitable to decision making.

1-7. Course Length

The primary premise of the ISA system of Independent Learning Modules is that students learn best if they proceed at their own pace. As a result, there will be significant variation in the amount of time taken by individual students to complete this ILM.

You are now ready to begin your in-depth study of measurement uncertainty. Please proceed to Unit 2.

Unit 2:
Fundamentals of Measurement Uncertainty Analysis

UNIT 2

Fundamentals of Measurement Uncertainty Analysis

This unit introduces measurement uncertainty analysis, including precision (or random error), standard deviation, and bias (or systematic error). Methods are given to estimate the magnitude of the effects of random errors and systematic errors.

Learning Objectives — When you have completed this unit, you should:

   A. Understand the purpose of engineering, experimental, or test measurements.

   B. Know the underlying principles of statistics as applied to measurement uncertainty analysis.

   C. Be able to characterize errors into either precision (random) or bias (systematic).

2-1. The Purpose of Engineering, Experimental, or Test Measurements

The purpose of measurements is the same whether they be engineering, experimental, or test measurements: to numerically characterize the state or performance of a physical process. Properly understanding the data obtained from such measurements is crucial to applying the knowledge thereby gained. The pressure to use test data for decision making is often so great that there is a tendency to assume the data is correct, even to the point of almost never reporting an estimate of the measurement uncertainty with its test result.

It is important to note that every measurement ever made by every engineer or scientist has been in error and will be so in the future. There has never been and never will be a case when a person measured a variable and obtained the *true* value. Error is the difference between the measurement and the true value.

However, there are several circumstances under which a measurement value is considered to be true. The most common is that value which supports the preconceived result expected by the measurer. This kind of data is frequently called "good data." Often the terms "right on," "nominal," "exact," "expected result," "astonishingly close," (my favorite) and so forth are applied to such test results. Conversely, "bad data" and "poor results" are terms often used to describe test results that do not support the action or conclusions wanted by the measurer. Each of those terms are subjective descriptions of the quality of test data or test results. They are ambiguous and as such should NEVER be used to describe the quality of a data set.

An objective, standardized method for describing and reporting the quality of test data or test results is needed. This ILM presents such an objective method. Measurement uncertainty analysis is a numerical, objective method for defining the potential that error exists in all data. The knowledge of the measurement uncertainty of a test result is as important as the result itself in characterizing the state or performance of a process. Test results should NEVER be reported without also reporting their measurement uncertainty. No manager or process owner should take action based on test results with an undefined measurement uncertainty.

The purpose of engineering, experimental, or test measurements is to develop enough knowledge about a process so that informed decisions can be made. Since all measurements are in error, a method must be employed to define just how much in error the measurements might be, as that will certainly affect the decisions made. This ILM provides such a method. It is a method that is accepted throughout the world by organizations such as the American Society of Mechanical Engineers (ASME) (1), the Instrument Society of America (ISA) and the US Air Force (2), Interagency Chemical Rocket Propulsion Group (ICRPG) (3), International Civil Aviation Organization (ICAO) (4), North Atlantic Treaty Organization (NATO) (5) and more. It should be noted that alternate approaches do exist. Chief among them is the approach of the International Standards Organization's (ISO) measurement uncertainty guidelines (unpublished 1992). The major concepts in this approach are outlined in Appendix H.

2-2. Measurement Error Definition

Early work by such visionaries as Churchill Eisenhart (6), Klein and McClintock (7), and others came to practical application and fruition with the work by Robert B. Abernethy when he contributed to the publication of the U. S. Air Force handbook on measurement uncertainty (2). That work was careful to divide error sources into two types: bias (or systematic) and precision (or random). The universally present third category, blunders (or mistakes), was assumed to be absent due to good engineering practice and so will it be in this ILM. However, it should be recognized that a careful, comprehensive uncertainty analysis will frequently uncover blunders that need to be corrected before a viable measurement system can operate properly.

Measurement uncertainty analysis is a function of the measurement system. It is necessary to completely define the measurement system before proceeding with an uncertainty analysis. After that definition, error sources may be treated as either precision or bias.

Precision or Random Error

General

In this section, the basics of statistics as applied to measurement uncertainty will be presented. The first major error type considered will be what is often called precision or random error.

Whenever a measurement is made, sources of precision or random error will add a component to the result that is unknown but, with repeated measurements, changes in a random fashion. That is, the error component added to the second measurement is uncorrelated to that which has been added to the first measurement. So it is with each successive measurement. Each has a random error component added, but none of the components are correlated. The errors may be related in the sense that they come from the same distribution but uncorrelated in the sense that errors in successive measurements cannot be forecast from a knowledge of errors in previous measurements.

Statistical Considerations

Random error components are drawn from a distribution of error that is Gaussian or normal. That is, the error components originate from a distribution that is described by the expression:

$$F(X) = \frac{1}{\sigma\sqrt{2\pi}}\, e^{-(X-\mu)^2/2\sigma^2} \qquad (2\text{-}1)$$

where:

μ = the population average
σ = the population standard deviation
X = a population value
F(X) = the frequency with which the value X occurs
e = the base of the natural logarithm

The value of σ is calculated for that distribution with the following expression:

$$\sigma = \lim_{n \to \infty} \{[\Sigma(X_i - \mu)^2/n]^{1/2}\} \qquad (2\text{-}2)$$

where:

Σ = Throughout this text, the Greek capital sigma, Σ, will be used as the summation sign over the index shown. In Eq. (2-2), the index is "i." In all other equations the summation index or indexes will be similarly obvious when they are not explicitly noted.
X_i = the ith data point extracted from the population
n = the number of data points used to calculate the standard deviation. Here, the number of data points in the population.

σ describes the scatter in the X values of the infinite population about its average, μ. It is also often called σ_X.

The effect of μ, σ (or σ_X), and n may be seen in Fig. 2-1.

Fig. 2-1 is a smooth curve. Its height above the horizontal axis of X values represents the relative frequency that the infinite population has at that X value, that X value's frequency of occurrence. Also illustrated is the area under the curve that is contained within the interval ($\mu \pm \sigma_X$). That area is $\cong 68\%$ of the total area under the curve. The interval ($\mu \pm 2\sigma_X$) contains $\cong 95\%$ of the area and ($\mu \pm 3\sigma_X$), $\cong 99.7\%$ of the area. The area under the curve is equal to the fraction of the population with values between the limits that define the area.

However, an experimenter never has all the data in the infinite population—only a sample of n data points with which to calculate the standard deviation. Nevertheless, for a data sample drawn from a Gaussian-normal distribution, the scatter

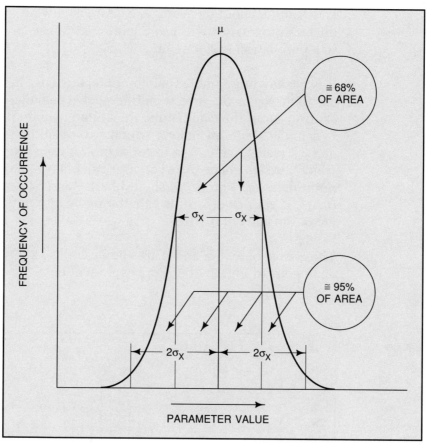

Fig. 2-1. Gaussian-Normal Distribution

in the data is characterized by the sample standard deviation, S_X.

$$S_X = \pm\{[\Sigma(X_i - \overline{X})^2/(n-1)]^{1/2}\} \qquad (2\text{-}3)$$

where:

X_i = the value of the ith X in the sample
$\overline{X}$ = the sample average
$(n-1)$ = the degrees of freedom for the sample.

Degrees of freedom (usually shown as ν) will be discussed in detail later.

Eq. (2-2) describes the scatter of an infinite set of data about the true population average, μ. Eq. (2-3) describes the scatter of a data sample about its average, $\overline{X}$. Almost always, the uncertainty analyst will use Equation (2-3) because all the data in a population is seldom available.

It is worthwhile to note that computers usually have a code to calculate S_X, as do most scientific pocket calculators. A word of caution about the calculators: they often contain the capability to calculate both S_X and σ_X, which are sometimes noted as σ_{n-1} and σ_n, respectively. The experimenter always wants S_X, so watch out. To check on what your calculator does, use the two-point data set, 1 and 2. $\overline{X}$ should be 1.5 and S_X should be 0.707. If your calculator is calculating σ_X instead of S_X, you will get 0.5 instead of 0.707.

The effects of $\overline{X}$, S_X, and n are shown in Fig. 2-2, which is analogous to Fig. 2-1 but for a sample of data.

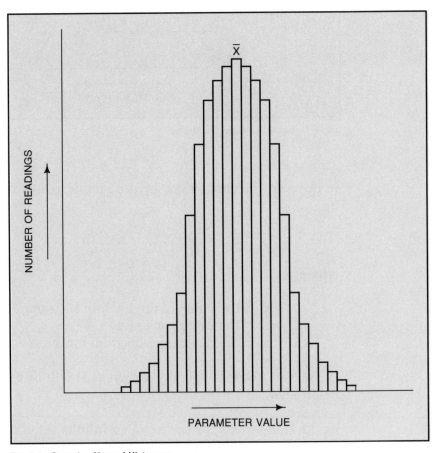

Fig. 2-2. Gaussian-Normal Histogram

Fig. 2-2 is actually a histogram of a large data sample (i.e., over 30 points). This plot is made so that the height of each bar represents the number of data points obtained in the interval shown by the width of the bar on the X axis. Here the interval $(\overline{X} \pm S_X)$ contains $\cong 68\%$ of the data sample, a situation similar to the infinite population but with $\overline{X}$ and S_X used rather than μ and σ_X. (This is also referred to as the 68% confidence interval.) Also, similarly, the interval $(\overline{X} \pm 2S_X)$ contains $\cong 95\%$ of the data and $(\overline{X} \pm 3S_X)$ contains $\cong 99.7\%$. When there are less than 31 data points (i.e., less than 30 degrees of freedom), the factors of $1S_X$, $2S_X$ and $3S_X$ change because of the "t statistic."

When there are less than 30 degrees of freedom, one, two, and three S_X are not the correct multipliers to be used to obtain the aforementioned $\cong 68\%$, $\cong 95\%$ and $\cong 99.7\%$ confidence. What is simple but only approximately correct is to use tS_X, where t is Student's "t." Appendix D contains the Student's "t" distribution for 95% confidence. Many texts (8) on statistics contain Student's "t" for other confidences, but those tables are usually not needed for experimental uncertainty analysis. This text uses the notation "t" to mean "$t_{95,\nu}$," where the 95 is used to represent 95% confidence and where ν is the degrees of freedom.

It is necessary to use Student's "t" to compensate for the tendency to calculate sample standard deviations that are smaller than the population standard deviation, when small samples of data are used. Here, small data samples means less than 31 data points. Consider Fig. 2-1; there is a great probability that a sample of only three or four data points will come from the center portion of the distribution, within $(\overline{X} \pm S_X)$. This would result in the calculation of too small a standard deviation to properly represent the population as a whole. The same tendency is true of larger samples, although with decreasing likelihood of underestimating the population standard deviation as the number of data points in the sample increases. Consulting the table in Appendix D, we note that once the degrees of freedom reach 30 (the number of data points reach 31), we may approximate "t" with 2.0 with no significant loss in accuracy in any uncertainty statement. Student's "t" is also needed to properly predict the distribution of replicate averages, but that will be covered later.

One of the most elusive concepts in uncertainty analysis is a definition of "degrees of freedom" (d.f. or ν). Texts in statistics are often either silent or presume too complex an understanding of statistics for the typical measurements specialist. Reference 9 provides such a detailed discussion. This text defines "degrees of freedom" as the freedom left in a data set for error or variability. For each constant calculated from a data set, one degree of freedom is lost. (It is presumed that the data comes from a uniform random population.) Therefore, since the average, $\overline{X}$, is first calculated to obtain S_X, one constant has been calculated, $\overline{X}$, and there is a loss of one degree of freedom in the calculation of S_X.

Sometimes $\overline{X}$ and S_X are called the first and second moments of the distribution of the data. For a detailed discussion of moments, consult Reference 10.

This "loss of freedom for variability" is sometimes easier to visualize when one considers a straight line fit to a data set, a

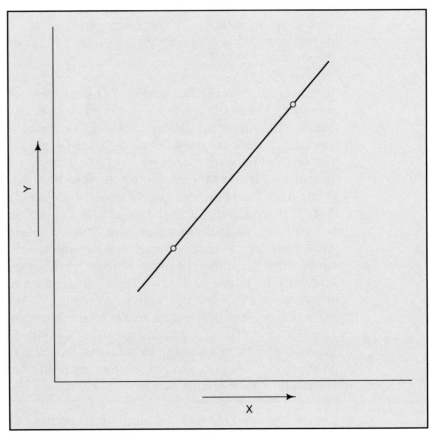

Fig. 2-3. Two-Point Line Fit

subject to be discussed in some detail in Unit 7. For now, consider a two-point data set as shown in Fig. 2-3.

Fig. 2-3 shows that a line fit to two data points will of necessity go through both points exactly. Two points define a line. There is no freedom in the data set for any error in the line fit. The line hits both points exactly. Since a straight line fit has two constants,

$$Y = aX + b \qquad (2\text{-}4)$$

two degrees of freedom are lost for each calculation of a straight line. Since there are only two data points, and since one degree of freedom is lost for each constant calculated, no degrees of freedom are left for error in the straight line fit. The line goes exactly through the two data points.

Now consider the fit shown in Fig. 2-4.

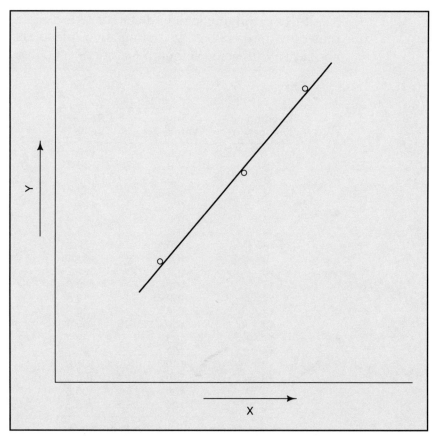

Fig. 2-4. Three-Point Line Fit

In Fig. 2-4 are three points to which a straight line has been fit. Note that not one of the data points is exactly on the line. Some error remains in describing the line. The degrees of freedom here is one (1)—three data points minus two constants calculated. The freedom left for error is shown in the scatter of the data about the line. Note that when there are degrees of freedom left, there is still room for error to show up from the calculated result—here, the straight line.

Remember, one degree of freedom is lost for each constant calculated from a data set.

Example 2-1:

To illustrate the computation and effect of $\overline{X}$, S_X, and tS_X, consider the sample of readings taken from a 4 by 5 array of thermocouples in a duct of rectangular cross section shown in Table 2-1. Note that here we assume that this data is normally distributed. If it were not, serious consequences would possibly result from applying standard statistical techniques of the type illustrated in this book. It is often advisable to check for normality with some standard technique, such as Bartlett's test.

Reading Number	True Value, F	Reading Value, F	Error, F
1	100.	100.5	0.5
2	100.	98.3	−1.7
3	100.	99.0	−1.0
4	100.	98.8	−1.2
5	100.	102.4	2.4
6	100.	101.3	1.3
7	100.	100.6	0.6
8	100.	99.6	−0.4
9	100.	101.1	1.1
10	100.	101.2	1.2
11	100.	100.3	0.3
12	100.	99.5	−0.5
13	100.	100.3	0.3
14	100.	99.9	−0.1
15	100.	99.0	−1.0
16	100.	99.7	−0.3
17	100.	101.8	1.8
18	100.	100.1	0.1
19	100.	100.5	0.5
20	100.	99.3	−0.7

Table 2-1. Thermocouple Data from Rectangular Duct

For the data sample in Table 2-1:

$$\overline{X} = 100.16$$
$$S_X = 1.06$$
$$n = 20$$
$$\nu = 19$$

From Appendix D we obtain t = 2.093

The data in Table 2-1 has an average of 100.16F and a standard deviation of 1.06F. This means that, on the average, approximately 95% of the data should be contained in the interval $(\overline{X} \pm tS_X)$ = [100.16 ± (2.093 × 1.06)] = (100.16 ± 2.22), or from 102.38 to 97.94. (Remember that this is only an approximate interval. For a complete discussion of confidence intervals, tolerance intervals, and prediction intervals, see Reference 11.) Reviewing the data, we find that one data point, number 5, is outside those limits. 95% of the data is inside the interval described by $(\overline{X} \pm tS_X)$. This is what we would expect! Amazing, it works!

A histogram of 5 segments may be constructed for the data in Table 2-1 as follows.

Choose the segments so that the low side of the bottom segment and the high side of the top segment include all the data. For 5 segments, divide the range of the data by 5 and round up to the nearest 0.1F. The range of the data is the maximum minus the minimum, or 102.4 − 98.3 = 4.1. Divide 4.1 by 5 to obtain 0.8^+ and round up to 0.9. Set up the segments, one centered on the average and two on each side of the average, 100.16, as shown in Table 2-2, and note the number of data points in each segment, the frequency.

Segment Number	Segment Interval, F	Frequency
1	97.91 − 98.81	2
2	98.81 − 99.71	6
3	99.71 − 100.61	7
4	100.61 − 101.51	3
5	101.51 − 102.41	2

Table 2-2. Histogram Data

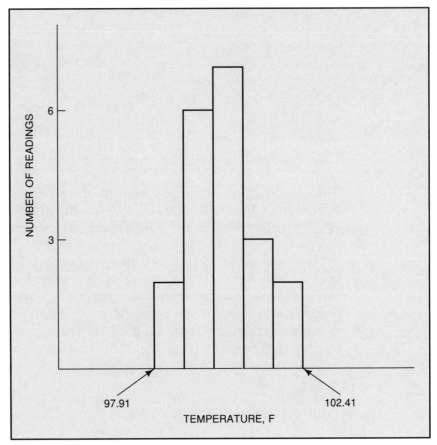

Fig. 2-5. Histogram of Data in Table 2-1

Fig. 2-5 is a histogram of the data in Table 2-1.

Note that there are not many bars because we only had 20 data points. It still can be seen, however, that the shape approximates the normal curve in Fig. 2-1. The 95% confidence interval approximation is noted as ($\overline{X} \pm tS_X$). The height of each bar is the frequency with which data in that interval occurs. On a smooth curve for an infinite population as shown in Fig. 2-1, the height of the curve is representative of the relative frequency with which that value shown on the X-axis occurs in the population.

Reviewing, we note that $\pm tS_X$ for a data set approximates the scatter of that data around its average, $\overline{X}$. S_X is the standard deviation of the data. $\pm tS_X$ is used with $\overline{X}$ to describe the interval, $\overline{X} \pm tS_X$, in which approximately 95% of the data will fall. $\pm tS_X$ is sometimes called the precision error for a particular data set.

Note that in the example S_X has been used in a generic sense; no specific subscripts have been used to identify a particular error source.

Having now understood the calculation of the standard deviation and the utility of the value tS_X, it is important to note that usually a measurement is taken to understand the average of the set of data, not the spread or scatter in the data. What is usually needed or wanted is a statement about the error present in the average $\overline{X}$.

That desire may be expressed by asking, "How good is the average?" Since the term "good" is poorly defined conceptually and undefined numerically, it would be more proper to ask, "Were the experiment to be repeated numerous times, thus securing many averages, how much scatter would be expected in those averages?"

Although the second question is the right one, one almost never has the opportunity to obtain the "many" averages. The next best question is, "May the expected scatter in many averages be estimated from the data set already obtained with its one average?" The answer here is yes, and the approach is to utilize the central limit theorem. Reference 12 gives an excellent discussion of the statistical derivation of the central limit theorem. It is sufficient for uncertainty analysis to note that the following is true: the expected standard deviation of many averages derived from an infinite population of a continuous, Gaussian random variable may be estimated as follows:

$$S_{\overline{X}} = S_X / \sqrt{N} \qquad (2\text{-}5)$$

where:

$S_{\overline{X}}$ = the standard deviation of the average, $\overline{X}$
N = the number of X_i being averaged

Here the standard deviation of a set of averages is seen to be estimated from the standard deviation of the data, S_X. For the case in which the true population standard deviation is known, σ_X, the true standard deviation of the population average, $\sigma_{\overline{X}}$, is calculated as $\sigma_{\overline{X}} = \sigma/\sqrt{N}$. In the case of a data sample, however, $S_{\overline{X}}$ is how much scatter could be expected in a group of averages were they available from the population from which our one data set has been drawn.

Now the expression $tS_{\overline{X}}$ may be considered. $tS_{\overline{X}}$ may be thought of as "How good is the average obtained?" Or, 95% of the time, the population average will be contained within the interval $(\overline{X} \pm tS_{\overline{X}})$.

Note in Eq. (2-5) that N may be different from the n used to calculate the S_X. If S_X is from historical data with lots of data points (many degrees of freedom), n will be very large (>30). The number of data points in an average is N, which is determined by the data sample averaged. (Sometimes, historical data bases provide a better data set from which to calculate S_X than the sample averaged.)

$tS_{\overline{X}}$ is often called the precision of the average for a particular data set or sample. If there is only one error source, it is also the random error component of the uncertainty or precision error.

The impact of $tS_{\overline{X}}$ may be seen in Fig. 2-6.

While 95% of the data will be contained in the interval $\overline{X} \pm 2S_X$ (for large sample sizes), it would also be expected that 95% of the time, the population average, μ, would be contained in the interval $\overline{X} \pm 2S_{\overline{X}}$. Note that, as shown in Fig. 2-6, the expected scatter in X, S_X, is always larger than the expected scatter in $\overline{X}$, $S_{\overline{X}}$.

Recalling that the data in Table 2-1 yielded an $\overline{X} = 100.16$ and an $S_X = 1.06$ with 20 data points, the estimate of the standard deviation of the average, $S_{\overline{X}}$, is:

$$S_{\overline{X}} = S_X/\sqrt{N} = 1.06/\sqrt{20} = 0.24 \qquad (2\text{-}6)$$

Here, n = N = 20.

From Eq. (2-6) it is then noted that the interval $\overline{X} \pm tS_{\overline{X}}$ contains the true average for the population, μ, 95% of the time. That is [100.16 $\pm$ (2.093 $\times$ 0.24)] or 100.16 $\pm$ 0.50 should contain the true average of the population from which the data set was drawn. Since the data set in Table 2-1 came

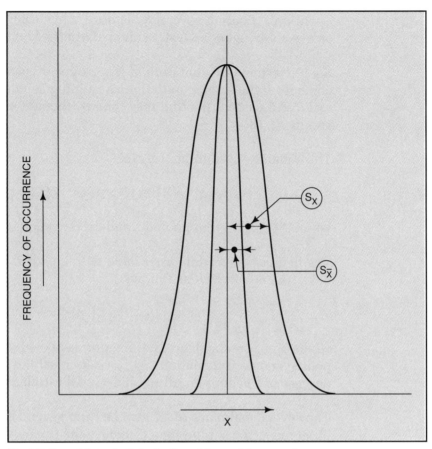

Fig. 2-6. Normal Curve for Data, S_X; Normal Curve of Averages, $S_{\bar{X}}$

from a population with $\sigma_X = 0.000$ and $\mu = 100.0$, it is noted that the interval does indeed contain the true average for the population.

Since the interval contains the true average, it might also be stated that the true average temperature is in the interval quoted. In an actual experimental situation, it would not be known whether the true value was above or below the average obtained, only that it was probably contained in the stated interval $\bar{X} \pm tS_{\bar{X}}$.

It should be noted that up to now only one estimate of the standard deviation has been discussed. There are times when several such estimates are available and one needs to consider which to use. Although it is obvious that the standard deviation with the most data is the most reliable, one may obtain a better estimate of the population standard deviation by combining several individual estimates through a process known as "pooling." Pooling several S_X is done when each of them passes a homogeneity test, such as Bartlett's homogeneity test.

Such a test assures that each of the groups of data or samples come from the same population. Assuming such a test has been made and passed, pooling may then be thought as averaging variances, $(S_X)^2$.

The equation used to pool S_X is:

$$S_{X,\,pooled} = \{\Sigma[(S_X)_i^2 \times \nu_i]\}^{1/2}/\{\Sigma[\nu_i]\}^{1/2} \qquad (2\text{-}7)$$

where $S_{X,\,pooled}$ = the pooled standard deviation.

The degrees of freedom associated with a pooled standard deviation is obtained as follows:

$$\nu_{pooled} = \{\Sigma(\nu_i)\} \qquad (2\text{-}8)$$

where ν_{pooled} = the degrees of freedom associated with the pooled standard deviation, $S_{X,\,pooled}$. It is just the sum of the degrees of freedom for all the individual estimates of S_X.

The several estimates of S_X may be from several days of data observed in a gas pipe line. Consider the three days' variability observed in the flow of natural gas in a pipe line as shown in Table 2-3.

The best estimate of the standard deviation in the table, considering that no change is expected between days, is that for day 2 because it has the most data. However, the pooled estimate is better than any individual day's estimate. It is calculated as follows.

$$S_{X,\,pooled} = \{[(23^2 \times 5) + (19^2 \times 11) + (27^2 \times 8)]^{1/2}\}$$

$$/\{(5 + 11 + 8)^{1/2}\} \qquad (2\text{-}9)$$

$$= (111.6)/(4.90) = 22.8$$

Day	Standard Deviation, ft^3	ν
1	23	5
2	19	11
3	27	8

Table 2-3. Natural Gas Variability

The best estimate of the population standard deviation is 22.8. The degrees of freedom associated with that standard deviation are:

$$\nu_{pooled} = 5 + 11 + 8 = 24 \tag{2-10}$$

Pooling standard deviations from several samples of data results in a better overall estimate of the population's standard deviation with more degrees of freedom than any one calculated standard deviation from one sample of data.

Another method for estimating the standard deviation expected for an instrument or measurement system is to compare the readings taken at the same time on a process with identical instruments. Even if the process varies, as long as the instruments are observing the same process parameter (that is, the same level) at the same time, their difference may be used to infer the standard deviation of one instrument. S_X is computed with the following equation:

$$S_X = \{[\Sigma(\Delta_i - \overline{\Delta})^2]/[2(n - 1)]\}^{1/2} \tag{2-11}$$

where:

Δ_i = the ith difference between the two measurements
$\overline{\Delta}$ = the average difference between the two measurements
n = the number of Δ_i used to calculate S_X

When using Eq. (2-11), only the differences between the two instruments are needed. The level does not enter the calculation.

Systematic Error or Bias

The Requirements for Accurate Measurements

When making a measurement, it is not sufficient to work toward small precision errors, small standard deviations, for the data. An accurate result requires small precision errors, but small precision errors do not guarantee small measurement uncertainty, the basic requirement for accurate measurements. Figs. 2-7 through 2-10 illustrate that point.

Fig. 2-7 shows a series of arrow strikes on a target where all the arrows have struck close together in the center of the target.

Fig. 2-7. Tight Arrows, Centered

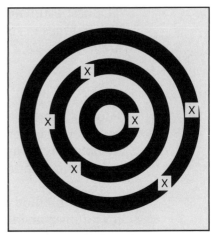

Fig. 2-8. Spread Arrows, Centered

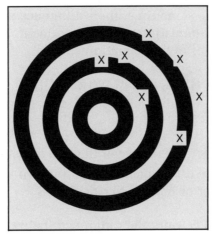

Fig. 2-9. Spread Arrows, Off Center

Fig. 2-10. Tight Arrows, Off Center

There is low precision error and low uncertainty. All the arrows are where they are supposed to be. The archer has been accurate. There is no systematic error of significance. For a measurement system, this is the most desirable result and will be assumed to have occurred because of the low precision error observed. We shall see later that this is a false sense of security.

Fig. 2-8 illustrates the situation wherein the archer has scattered his arrow hits greatly but still centered them on the target. The precision is poor but, on the average, the accuracy is acceptable. There is still no significant systematic error. An experimenter will notice here the broad scatter, decide the measurement system is inadequate, and work to improve it.

However, that decision will be made solely based on the scatter observed and not on the fact that unobservable systematic error also may exist.

Fig. 2-9 is the case in which the arrows are scattered far and wide and are well off the center of the target. Here the archer really needs help! The precision is poor and systematically to the right. Some systematic error or bias shows in the impact pattern of the arrows. In a measurement system, the experimenter will often recognize this situation as unacceptable, not because it is off target but because there is so much scatter in the results. (Note that with modern data acquisition systems, the data may be rapidly averaged and only the average displayed. The experimenter will thus have no idea that there is a large precision error.) Improvement in the experimental method is needed.

Fig. 2-10 illustrates the arrows tightly grouped but off the center of the target. This is the most dangerous situation of all for an experimenter. The archer can see that the arrows are off center; the experimenter cannot. The experimenter assumes the center of the target (true value for the measurement) is the center of the data (center of the arrows). There is low precision error here, but this is not a sufficient condition to assure low uncertainty. This archer, and, analogously, the experimenter, has significant bias. The archer can see it. The experimenter never can. The experimenter can see only the test data (the location of the arrows), not the true test result (the target).

It is necessary, therefore, to include in uncertainty analysis the second major error type, systematic error or bias.

Definition and Effect of Systematic Error or Bias

Systematic error and bias are constant for the duration of the experiment. Bias affects every measurement of a variable the same amount. It is not observable in the test data. The archer above could see there is bias in the aiming system because the target can be seen. However, remember that the experimenter does not see the target but assumes the center has been hit with the average of the measurements. Further, it is the insidious nature of bias that, when there is low precision error, one assumes the measurement is accurate, low uncertainty. This is not a sufficient condition for an accurate measurement. Precision and bias errors must both be low.

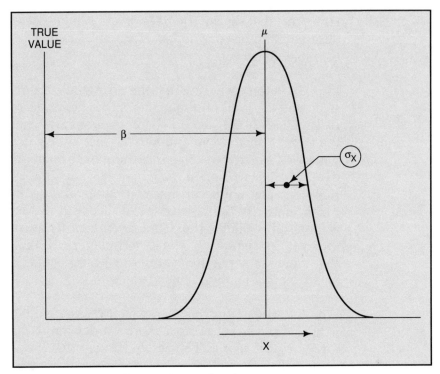

Fig. 2-11. Normal Curve Displaced from the True Value

Fig. 2-11 illustrates the effect of bias and precision errors.

Since the true bias error, β, is never known, its limits must be estimated with the bias limit, B. Note that in Fig. 2-11 the scatter around the biased average is shown to be illustrated by σ_X. The difference between the biased average and the true value is β. As B is an estimator of the limits of β, we note that β is contained in the interval $-B \leq \beta \leq +B$; so, the bias limit is expressed as $\pm B$.

Five Types of Bias Errors

There are five types of bias errors. These are summarized in Table 2-4.

Bias errors of type 1 are large errors known to exist, and an experimenter calibrates them out. Examples include pressure transducer calibrations, thermocouple calibrations, volt meter calibrations, and the like. In each case, it is known that data of unacceptably large error will be obtained from such an instrument unless it is calibrated. The calibration process trades

Size	Known Sign and Magnitude	Unknown Magnitude
Large	1. Calibrated out	3. Assumed to be eliminated
Small	2. Negligible contribution to bias limit	4. Unknown sign 5. Known sign

Table 2-4. Five Types of Bias Error

the large error of not calibrating for the (assumed) small errors of the calibration process.

Bias errors of type 2 are known to exist but are assessed as being small enough that they don't influence the outcome of the test measurement. One example might be the thermal conductivity of a thermocouple in a process stream. Such conductivity-caused bias error may be deemed negligible for the test in question. If those errors are deemed negligible, they don't enter an uncertainty analysis. However, be careful here as errors assumed to be negligible are not always so. Prudent judgment is needed.

Bias errors of type 3 are large errors that are assumed to be properly engineered out of the experiment or test. An example might be the proper use of flow straighteners in front of a turbine meter. Without those straighteners, swirl in the stream will cause the meters to read in error. The proper engineering practice of setting up the test, instrumentation, and data recording is deemed adequate to eliminate errors of this type. It should be noted that although these bias errors do not have a part in uncertainty analysis, if they still exist in the measurement system, their presence often will be made known by the existence of data that is difficult to explain.

Bias errors of types 4 and 5 are included in an uncertainty analysis. These bias errors are of unknown magnitude but are not eliminated by engineering practice, not corrected out by calibration and not negligible. If their signs are not known, they are expressed by the bias limit term $\pm B$ in the uncertainty analysis. If the sign of the error has a known tendency, either positive or negative, is it necessary in uncertainty analysis to carry through two bias error terms, $-B^-$ and $+B^+$. These represent the positive and negative estimates of a particular bias error source. Nonsymmetrical bias limits will be detailed in Unit 3.

Obtaining Estimates of Bias Errors

Since bias errors are not known but only estimated, the term used to describe the limit likely for a bias error is "bias limit." Coming up with an estimate of the magnitude for a bias error source is often difficult. Reference 12 provides five methods for obtaining bias error limits.

Method 1—Tests with artifacts or samples run at several laboratories or facilities will do a fine job in estimating bias error between facilities. The scatter in that data, usually expressed as $\pm tS_X$ may be used to express the bias for one facility or laboratory. This is because that one facility is assumed to be constantly different from the group whose spread is $\pm tS_X$, where X represents the several facilities or laboratories whose measurements are compared. The facility cannot correct its data to the average since, in a properly run intercomparison, facilities are not identified. If they are identified, corrections should still not be applied, as the spread is real evidence of bias in the method and it affects each facility.

Method 2—Where possible, an estimate of an instrument's bias may be obtained by transporting a calibration standard to the instrument in its operating environment. Numerous comparisons of this type will yield an estimate of the typical bias for that instrument in its application. These tests could also be used to calibrate the instrument and remove that bias error source if so desired. It is important to remember, however, that to continue that loss of a source of error requires continued in-place calibration.

Method 3—There are times when several independent methods are available to measure the same thing. For instance, jet engine air flow may be measured with the inlet bellmouth (nozzle), the compressor speed-flow map, the turbine flow parameter, and the exhaust nozzle discharge coefficient. Each of these may be configured to be independent measurements. The differences observed (in the average) are evidences of the bias errors of the methods. The bias for any one method may be estimated by $\pm tS_X$ as in method 1 of Table 2-4 where X represents the several measurement methods.

Method 4—When it is known that there are specific causes for bias error, special calibrations can be run to eliminate that error source. Failing that, repeated calibrations can estimate its magnitude for inclusion in the uncertainty analysis.

Method 5—When all else fails, one can use the judgment of several competent experimenters to estimate the bias limits. Beware of pride here. Many experimenters will start out by saying their experiments have no bias. This is never true and a reasonable, careful, thoughtful estimate can be had. One can use instrument manufacturers' literature with care as these represent the judgments of those producing the device for sale.

2-3. Summary

Besides precision, bias errors must be estimated for a complete uncertainty analysis. It is difficult but necessary. Their combination into uncertainty will be covered later.

References

1. ANSI/ASME PTC 19.1-1985, *Instruments and Apparatus, Part 1, Measurement Uncertainty.*
2. Abernethy, R. B., et al., *Handbook—Gas Turbine Measurement Uncertainty,* AEDC, 1973.
3. *ICRPG Handbook for Estimating the Uncertainty in Measurements Made with Liquid Propellant Rocket Engine Systems,* Chemical Propulsion Information Agency, No. 180, 30 April 1969.
4. "Assessment of Uncertainty in the Calibration and Use of Flow Measurement Devices, Part 1, Linear Calibration Relationships," *ISO/DIS 7066-1.2,* 1988-04-28 and "Part 2, Nonlinear Calibration Relationships," *ISO 7066-2,* 1988-07-01.
5. "Recommended Practice for Measurement of Gas Path Pressures and Temperatures for Performance Assessment of Turbine Engines and Components," *NATO AGARD Advisory Report No. 245,* pp. 35–41, June 1990.
6. Eisenhart, C., "Realistic Evaluation of the Precision and Accuracy of Instrument Calibration Systems," *Journal of Research of the NBS,* vol. 67C, no. 2, April–June 1963.
7. Klein, S. J., and McClintock, F. A., "Describing Uncertainty in Single-Sample Experiments," *Mechanical Engineering,* vol. 75, p. 308, Jan. 1973.
8. Bowker, A. H., and Lieberman, E. H., *Experimental Statistics,* p. 603 (Prentice-Hall, 1969).
9. *Ibid.,* pp. 114–116.

10. Mendenhall, W., and Scheaffer, R. L., *Mathematical Statistics with Applications*, pp. 299–302 (Doxbury Press, 1973).
11. Hahn, G., "Understanding Statistical Intervals," *Industrial Engineering*, December, 1970.
12. *Ibid.*, pp. 252–256.

Exercises:

2-1. Student t Problems

    a. Write the expression for the standard deviation of the average as a function of the standard deviation of the data.

    b. Write the expression for the random error component of uncertainty, sometimes called the precision of the average or result.

    c. In your own words, describe what the equation of (b) above means with reference to replicate samples of $\overline{X}$.

    d. Given $\overline{X} = 4.9$ $S_X = 1.7$ d.f. = 11

        1) Calculate the random error component of uncertainty (precision of the average or result).

        2) Write the interval that will contain μ, the true average, 95% of the time.

2-2. Pooling Problems

Assume appropriate homogeneity tests are met.
Consider the following five estimates of the same σ:

S_X	325	297	301	280	291
ν	15	12	22	3	7

    a. What is the best estimate of σ in the above?

    b. Calculate the random error component of the uncertainty (precision of the average or result) for each case.

    c. A pooled S_X is better than any one S_X. Calculate $S_{X,\text{pooled}}$ and ν_{pooled}.

2-3. Dependent Calibration Problems

A gasoline refinery decides to add a second volumetric flowmeter in series to each of the input and output fluid lines in an effort to improve accuracy (reduce uncertainty).

    a. Should the flowmeters be calibrated simultaneously or separately?

b. *How would you decide if an independent metrology laboratory should be contracted to calibrate one or both meters?*
c. *Only one determination of fluid density is available for each pair of meters. What effect does this have on the two measured weight flows in each line?*
d. *What is the best estimate of the flow through the refinery if we assume no losses?*

Unit 3:
The Measurement Uncertainty Model

UNIT 3

The Measurement Uncertainty Model

In this unit, the procedures and models will be developed for providing the decision makers a clear, unambiguous statement of the accuracy or uncertainty of their data. No manager should ever be without a statement of measurement uncertainty attendant upon each piece of data on which decisions are based. No experimenter should permit management to consider measurement data without also considering its measurement uncertainty. The manager has the responsibility for requiring measurement uncertainty statements. The experimenter has the responsibility for never reporting test results without also reporting their measurement uncertainty.

Learning Objectives — When you have completed this unit, you should:

A. Understand the need for a single-valued uncertainty statement.

B. Be able to characterize error sources as bias or precision.

C. Be able to combine elemental bias and elemental precision errors into the bias limit and precision index for the measurement process.

D. Be able to combine the bias limit and precision index into a single value of measurement uncertainty for the measurement process.

3-1. The Statement of Measurement Uncertainty

The purpose of measurements is to numerically characterize the state or performance of a physical process. Properly understanding the data from measurements requires a statement of uncertainty.

In the previous unit, the concepts of systematic error (bias) and random error (precision) were developed. It is not enough to be able to state the bias and precision of a measurement. Management decision makers neither understand nor want to understand the intricacies of uncertainty analysis. They do *not* want to hear a flow level is 3000 scfm with ± 30 scfm bias, ± 14 scfm precision with 75 degrees of freedom. That's too much thinking for a manager who still remembers slide rules and who wants (and should require) a single number from which to understand the limits of accuracy for the 3000 scfm measurement. That single number is the statement of *measurement uncertainty*. It is a single, unambiguous number.

3-2. Grouping and Categorizing Error Sources

To conduct a proper uncertainty analysis, it is necessary to identify the error sources that affect an experimental result and to characterize them as *bias (systematic)* or *precision (random)*. In addition, the bookkeeping process is eased when the error sources are grouped into categories (1). It is instructive to group error sources into four categories: *calibration, data acquisition, data reduction, and errors of method.*

Grouping Error Sources

Calibration errors are those that result from the laboratory certification of an instrument response. Usually, this category includes those errors that result from the use of instruments at the test site (sometimes called installation errors). It is very important to note that these are not the usual calibration errors that are calibrated out by the calibration process. For example, it may be known that a pressure transducer will have an uncertainty of $\pm 2.0\%$ if it is not calibrated and $\pm 0.5\%$ when it is. In this case, the large known bias ($\pm 2\%$) has been traded for the smaller errors in the calibration process ($\pm 0.5\%$). Error sources totaling $\pm 1.5\%$ have been removed. What remains is the unknown error of the calibration process. Only its limits are known: $\pm 0.5\%$. It is this $\pm 0.5\%$ that will enter the uncertainty analysis (properly split between bias and precision). These errors are determined by a careful uncertainty analysis of the instrument calibration and use process.

Data acquisition errors are those that result from the use of data acquisition equipment, which may be computer data acquisition systems, a data logger, or just a person with pencil and paper reading a meter. Acquiring data to estimate the magnitude of these error sources is usually simple. All that is needed is to take multiple readings over the appropriate time period. This category of errors is also usually smaller in magnitude than calibration errors by a factor of three to ten. As with calibration errors, the exact magnitude of these errors is not known; only their limits for both bias and precision are known.

Data reduction errors are those that most often result from the use of computers or pocket calculators. Truncation, roundoff, and approximate solutions are examples in this category. These error sources are usually smaller than either of the former two sources, but they can be significant. The most common reason that these errors are significant is improper curve fitting, which will be discussed in Unit 7.

Errors of method is a new category not considered in Reference 1. These errors are sometimes called personal errors. They have to do with the ability of the experimenter to adjust instruments on the test site. Sometimes this group also includes sampling error, that is, how well a measurement system is characterized considering its own variability or profiles. Sampling error is discussed in Unit 7.

Grouping errors into categories is not a necessary step to a correct uncertainty analysis. It is only a bookkeeping aid. (It is fully correct to conduct an uncertainty analysis with only one big group for all the error sources.)

Note: Units 3 and 4 present the calculation of measurement uncertainty for a single measurement or parameter such as temperature or pressure. When these measurements are then used to calculate a result, such as flow, the systematic and random errors must be propagated into that result, using the methods of Unit 5.

Categorizing Errors

Early on in an uncertainty analysis it is necessary to decide whether an error source is bias or precision. The defined measurement system will provide the information necessary to make this choice. But there are times when the same error source is a bias in one circumstance and a precision in another. For example, in a multifacility test, the scatter between facilities would be a precision error ($\pm X\%$) if one were describing facility-to-facility variability. However, from the perspective of working in only one facility, that same data scatter indicates that one facility could be biased compared to the others by an amount within the interval of $\pm X\%$. The exact same error source is on one occasion precision and on another bias, depending on the context of the test.

The following is the best rule to use: *If an error source causes scatter in the test result, it is a precision (or random) error. All other error sources are bias (or systematic) errors.* This is without regard to the source of error. The emphasis here is on the *effect* of the error source. It does not matter where the error comes from; it matters where it's going—its effect. What matters is what effect the error source has on the manager's ability to make decisions with the test results. Errors have the effect of inhibiting proper decisions or, worse, selling a faulty product. Bias errors, while invisible in test data, will cause an entire test program to be off from the true value. Precision errors, their effects always visible in the test data, will cause scatter in the test results—always, by definition.

Categorizing error sources, therefore, is simply utilizing the above rule. It works in every case. It ignores origins. It considers what most experimenters want to know: What does it do to the data or test result? This view allows one to apply the knowledge to the decision-making process that follows an experiment.

Designating Error Sources

A subscripted notation for error sources is described in Reference 1. The general notation for an elemental bias error source is b_{ij}, where b_{ij} is the bias limit estimate for the ith elemental error source in the jth category. Similarly, the notation for an elemental precision error source (standard deviation) is s_{ij}, where s_{ij} is the standard deviation of the data from the ith error source in the jth category. These i and j subscripts will be utilized throughout this text to designate error sources in categories, respectively.

3-3. The Calculation of Measurement Uncertainty (Symmetrical Bias Limits)

Combining Precision Errors

It is informative to note that there is no need to determine the effect of combined precision errors once a test has been run. The scatter in the data is exactly the right effect of all the precision errors! However, before scarce dollars are spent on a test program, it is important to know whether or not the results will be useful. In this important case, it is necessary to do a pretest uncertainty analysis as discussed in Unit 4. In this section, the methods for combining the effects of several error sources will be delineated. This combination is a requirement for understanding the expected uncertainty of a test before it is run.

The Standard Deviation of the Elemental Error Sources

The first level of precision error is the elemental error. This is the precision of the data caused by each error source. The equation for the elemental precision errors is:

$$s_{ij} = \pm\{[\Sigma(X_{ijk} - \overline{X}_{ij})^2/(n - 1)]^{1/2}\} \qquad (3\text{-}1)$$

Note: The sum is over k where there are n_{ij} values of X_{ijk}.

Here, s_{ij} is the standard deviation of elemental error source i in category j. The standard deviation is calculated exactly as in Eq. (3-1). If this were the only precision error source, the test data would exhibit scatter identical to that described by s_{ij}.

However, there is always more than one error source, and it is necessary to combine their effects when estimating what the precision error for an experiment might be. Having combined them, it is necessary to estimate the appropriate degrees of freedom. The first step in this combination is the calculation of the precision index for an error source.

The Precision Index for an Error Source

What matters most about an error source is its average effect for a particular experimental result. Seldom does one care what the actual data scatter might be. One is always concerned about its average effect. In fact, test results are almost always reported as the average for the data obtained. The effect on the average for a particular elemental precision error may be expressed as:

$$S_{ij} = \pm[s_{ij}/(N_{ij})^{1/2}] \qquad (3\text{-}2)$$

where:

S_{ij} = the *precision index* (or standard error of the mean) for error source i in category j

N_{ij} = the number of data points averaged for error source i, j

This is an outgrowth of the central limit theorem (2). What is being done here is to estimate the precision of the average from the precision of the data. Note that N_{ij} may or may not equal n_{ij}, as explained in Unit 2.

What is most important is the effect that an elemental precision error source has on the average value. Stated another way, what would the precision of a group of averages be for a particular error source? Usually, there is neither time nor money to run numerous experiments so that many averages can be obtained. It is necessary, therefore, to estimate what that distribution of averages would be: what the precision of that group of averages would be. That estimate is achieved with Eq. (3-2), where the precision of the data is used to estimate the precision of the average for a particular elemental precision error source.

The Precision Index for the Result (the Random Error Component of the Uncertainty)

It is then the combined effect of the several precision indices on the average for the test or the test result that needs evaluation. That combined effect is determined by Eq. (3-3).

$$S = \pm[\Sigma\Sigma\,(S_{ij})^2]^{1/2} \qquad (3\text{-}3)$$

where S and S_{ij} have the same units. Note the double sum is over both i and j. It is the S_{ij} values that are root sum squared, not the s_{ij} values. This is an important fact to be remembered in the rest of this text.

It is S, the *precision index for the result*, that forms the basis for the *uncertainty statement*.

It is important to note that $t_{95}S$ is the random error component of the uncertainty statement. There will be more on this later.

Combining Degrees of Freedom

In order to utilize the correct t_{95} in an uncertainty statement, it is necessary to know the correct degrees of freedom, ν, associated with the *precision index of the result*, S. Each of the elemental error sources has its associated degrees of freedom, ν_{ij}. The same degrees of freedom, ν_{ij}, are associated with the corresponding precision index for the error source S_{ij}. When the S_{ij} are combined with Eq. (3-3), it is necessary to combine

degrees of freedom as well. References 3 and 4 utilize the
Welch-Satterthwaite approximation given originally in
Reference 5. There, the degrees of freedom for a test result are
given as:

$$\nu = \frac{[\Sigma\Sigma(S_{ij})^2]^2}{\{\Sigma\Sigma[(S_{ij})^4/\nu_{ij}]\}} \tag{3-4}$$

Note the double sum over i and j.

It should be noted that the degrees of freedom for any step
along the way to an uncertainty analysis is also obtainable. For
instance, Eq. (3-4) is the degrees of freedom for the first error
category—calibration where j = 1.

$$\nu_1 = \frac{[\Sigma(S_{i1})^2]^2}{\{\Sigma[(S_{i1})^4/\nu_{i1}]\}} \tag{3-5}$$

Note this is a single sum over only i.

It may then be seen that for each error category, j, the values ν_1,
ν_2, ν_3, and ν_4 may be combined with S_1, S_2, S_3, and S_4 to obtain
the degrees of freedom identical to those obtained with Eq.
(3-2). The writing of the formulas for the S_j's is left as an
exercise for the reader (see Exercise 3-3). The degrees of
freedom may then be obtained as follows.

$$\nu = \frac{[\Sigma(S_j)^2]^2}{\{\Sigma[(S_j)^4/\nu_j]\}} \tag{3-6}$$

Here, each category, e.g., calibration, is evaluated first and the
results combined in Eq. (3-6).

Combining Symmetrical Bias Limits

Bias limits may be expressed as *symmetrical*, which is the first
case treated here, or *nonsymmetrical*, which will be presented
later.

Bias limits come from various error sources, and their
combined effect must be evaluated. This is true whether the
effect is to be noted in a pretest uncertainty analysis or a
posttest analysis. Remember, test data, while revealing the
magnitude and effect of precision errors, does not do so for bias

limits. One cannot see the effect of bias in test data. It must be estimated from the combined effect of various sources.

The Symmetrical Bias Limit for the Test Result

Each elemental bias limit, b_{ij}, must have its combined effect on the test result evaluated. That combined effect is determined by Eq. (3-7).

$$B = \pm[\Sigma\Sigma(b_{ij})^2]^{1/2} \qquad (3-7)$$

where B = the bias limit of the test result and where B and b_{ij} have the same units. Note the double sum is over i and j.

B is the basis for the bias error component of the uncertainty statement. It is the systematic error component, and it is the value used for the symmetrical bias limit.

Summarizing Error Categorization (Symmetrical Bias Limits)

Bias and precision error sources and their categories may be summarized as shown in Table 3-1.

Assuming that the values in Table 3-1 are the errors at the temperature calibration point of interest, the bias limit for the calibration is obtained as follows:

$$B_1 = \pm[\Sigma(b_{i1})^2]^{1/2}$$
$$= \pm[(0.5)^2 + (0.1)^2 + (0.2)^2]^{1/2} \qquad (3-8)$$
$$= \pm0.55\,°F$$

Error Sources (i)	°F Bias Limit (b_{i1})	°F Standard Deviation (s_{i1})	No. Data Points Avg'd. (N_{i1})*	°F Precision Index (S_{i1})	Degrees of Freedom (n − 1) (v_{i1})
(1) Intermediate thermocouple reference	0.5	0.055	1	0.055	29
(2) Ice reference junction	0.1	0.016	1	0.016	9
(3) Volt meter readout	0.2	0.1	5	0.045	4

*Number of data points averaged in this measurement. That is, 1 intermediate reference reading, 1 ice reference reading, and 5 voltmeter readings averaged for each temperature measurement.

Note: The degrees of freedom are associated with s_{i1} and S_{i1} and *not* N_{i1}.

Table 3-1. Temperature Calibration Error Sources, j = 1

Here, B_1 is used because the equation deals only with calibration errors where $j = 1$. For the same reason, there is only one summation over i because all errors here are category 1, calibration.

To obtain the precision index for this experiment, a similar root-sum-square approach is used as follows:

$$
\begin{aligned}
S_1 &= \pm[\Sigma(s_i/N_{i1}^{1/2})^2] \\
&= \pm[\Sigma(S_{i1})^2]^{1/2} \\
&= \pm[(0.055)^2 + (0.016)^2 + (0.045)^2]^{1/2} \\
&= \pm 0.073\,°F
\end{aligned}
\tag{3-9}
$$

To compute the uncertainty, it is necessary to obtain a t_{95} value from Appendix D. To do that, the appropriate degrees of freedom must be obtained. To obtain the degrees of freedom, the Welch-Satterthwaite approximation is used, Eq. (3-4).

$$
\nu_1 = \frac{[\Sigma(S_{i1})^2]^2}{\{\Sigma[(S_{i1})^4/\nu_{i1}]\}}
$$

$$
\nu_1 = \frac{[(0.055)^2 + (0.016)^2 + (0.045)^2]^2}{\dfrac{(0.055)^4}{29} + \dfrac{(0.016)^4}{9} + \dfrac{(0.045)^4}{4}}
$$

$$
= 21.1 = 21
$$

Note that, to obtain the correct degrees of freedom, 21.1 is truncated to 21. Were the algebraic value 21.9, the correct degrees of freedom would still have been 21. Always truncate, as this is the conservative value for the degrees of freedom. The evaluation of why this is conservative is left as an exercise for the reader (see Exercise 3-5).

Appendix D provides $t_{95} = 2.080$ for 21 degrees of freedom.

The information is now available to form an uncertainty statement.

3-4. The Uncertainty Statement (Symmetrical Bias Limits)

Measurement uncertainty is defined as the combination of both the systematic and random error components of uncertainty, bias and precision. Reference 3 provides two methods for that combination. Those methods are called the *addition* model and the *root-sum-square* model.

The Addition (ADD) Uncertainty Model

The *addition* uncertainty model is defined as:

$$U_{ADD} = \pm[B + t_{95}S] \qquad (3\text{-}10)$$

where U_{ADD} is the *additive uncertainty*.

U_{ADD} provides an interval (or coverage) around the test average that will contain the true value $\approx 99\%$ of the time (Reference 6). It is also called U_{99} for that reason. Stated another way, the true value, μ, is contained in the interval:

$$(\overline{X} - U_{ADD}) \le \mu \le (\overline{X} + U_{ADD}) \qquad (3\text{-}11)$$

approximately 99% of the time. This interval may also be written as:

$$(\overline{X} - U_{99}) \le \mu \le (\overline{X} + U_{99}) \qquad (3\text{-}12)$$

$$U_{ADD} = U_{99} \qquad (3\text{-}13)$$

The Root-Sum-Square (RSS) Uncertainty Model

The *root-sum-square* uncertainty model is defined as:

$$U_{RSS} = \pm[(B)^2 + (t_{95}S)^2]^{1/2} \qquad (3\text{-}14)$$

where U_{RSS} is the *root-sum-square uncertainty*.

U_{RSS} provides an interval around the test average that will contain the true value $\approx 95\%$ of the time (6). It is also called U_{95} for that reason. Stated another way, the true value, μ, is contained in the interval:

$$(\overline{X} - U_{RSS}) \le \mu \le (\overline{X} + U_{RSS}) \qquad (3\text{-}15)$$

approximately 95% of the time. This interval may also be written as:

$$(\overline{X} - U_{95}) \le \mu \le (\overline{X} + U_{95}) \qquad (3\text{-}16)$$

$$U_{RSS} = U_{95} \qquad (3\text{-}17)$$

3-5. Computing the Uncertainty Interval (Symmetrical Bias Limits)

The information is now available to compute the uncertainty interval, or measurement uncertainty, for the case in Table 3-1 with symmetrical bias limits. The values to be used are from Eqs. (3-8) and (3-9).

The U_{ADD} Uncertainty Interval (Symmetrical Bias Limits)

For the U_{ADD} uncertainty, the expression is:

$$U_{ADD} = \pm[B + t_{95}S]$$
$$= \pm[0.55 + (2.080 \times 0.073)]$$
$$= \pm[0.71]°F$$

Assuming an average calibration correction of $+2.00°F$ at the temperature of interest, it can be stated that the interval:

$$(2.00 - 0.71) \le \mu°F \le (2.00 + 0.71)$$
$$1.29 \le \mu°F \le 2.71$$
$$\mu = 2.00 \pm 0.71°F$$

contains the true value for the correction, μ, 99% of the time; that is, there is 99% coverage of the true value.

This coverage is shown schematically in Fig. 3-1 and specifically in Fig. 3-2.

In the interval shown in Fig. 3-2, the true value of the temperature calibration correction will be contained 95% of the time.

The U_{RSS} Uncertainty Interval (Symmetrical Bias Limits)

For the U_{RSS} uncertainty, the expression is (Eq. (3-14)):

$$U_{RSS} = \pm[B^2 + (t_{95}S)^2]^{1/2}$$
$$= [(0.55)^2 + (2.080 \times 0.073)^2]^{1/2}$$
$$= \pm[0.57]°F$$

Assuming an average calibration correction of $+2.00°F$ at the temperature of interest, it can be stated that the interval:

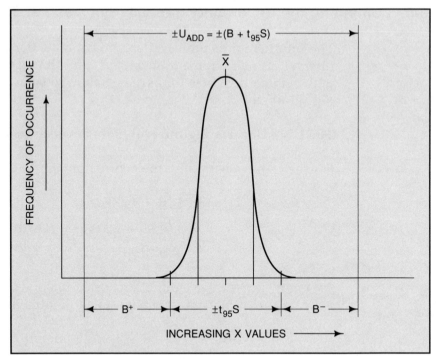

Fig. 3-1. U_{ADD} **Symmetrical Uncertainty Interval**

$$(2.00 - 0.57) \leq \mu°F \leq (2.00 + 0.57)$$

$$1.43 \leq \mu°F \leq 2.57$$

$$\mu = 2.00 \pm 0.57°F$$

contains the true value for the correction, μ, 95% of the time; that is, there is 95% coverage of the true value. This coverage is shown schematically in Fig. 3-1 where one merely replaces the term U_{ADD} with U_{RSS}.

In the interval shown in Fig. 3-1 with the use of U_{RSS}, the true value of the temperature calibration correction will be contained 95% of the time.

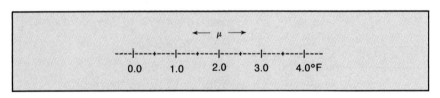

Fig. 3-2. **Uncertainty Interval for** $\mu = 2.00 \pm 0.71$

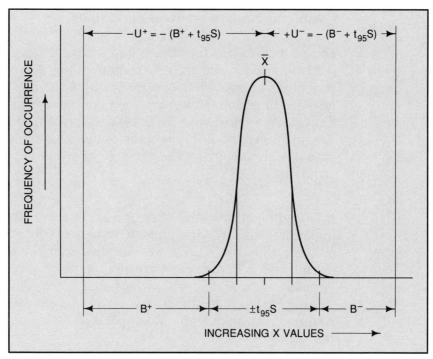

Fig. 3-3. U_{ADD} **Nonsymmetrical Uncertainty Interval**

The Choice of the Uncertainty Model

The uncertainty model should be chosen for the coverage desired. In some industries, such as aerospace, a great penalty is assessed if a wrong decision is made based on a test result. Therefore, the aerospace standard (7) utilized the U_{ADD} model that provides 99% coverage of the true value. The steam turbine world, however, prefers the 95% coverage of the U_{RSS} model.

The choice is up to the user, but the model chosen must be reported. For most examples, this text will use the more conservative approach: the U_{ADD} model.

3-6. The Calculation of Measurement Uncertainty (Nonsymmetrical Bias Limits)

The first step here is the proper handling of the nonsymmetrical bias limits.

Combining Nonsymmetrical Bias Limits

For most cases, the bias limits and the resulting uncertainty interval or measurement uncertainty will be symmetrical; that is, there is an equal risk of error in either the positive or the negative direction. However, there are times when the bias limit is not symmetrical. In these cases, something is known about the physics or engineering of the measurement that prompts a tendency for the errors to be either negative or positive.

An example of this kind of error might be a pressure reading from a transducer, which may tend to read low while trying to follow a ramp up in pressure. Another example might be a thermocouple in a process stream that, because of the laws of thermal conductivity, will always tend to read low when reading higher than ambient temperatures and high when reading lower than ambient temperatures.

Summarizing Error Categorization (Nonsymmetrical Bias Limits)

Suppose that, of the errors in Table 3-1, the NIST standard calibration bias limit was nonsymmetrical, in that the tendency was to read low for the higher than ambient calibration points. Given that the bias limit was nonsymmetrical as follows: -0.7 to $+0.3°F$, it is noted that the range of bias limit is still $1.0°F$. However, it is skewed negative. The error data then needs to be reformatted from Table 3-1 into Table 3-2.

Error Sources (i)	0°F Bias Limits (b_{i1}^-)	(b_{i1}^+)	0°F Standard Deviation (s_{i1})	No. Data Points Avg'd. (N_{i1})*	0°F Precision Index (S_{i1})	Degrees of Freedom (n − 1) (v_{i1})
(1) Intermediate TC reference	−0.7	+0.3	0.055	1	0.055	29
(2) Ice reference junction	−0.1	+0.1	0.016	1	0.016	9
(3) Voltmeter readout	−0.2	+0.2	0.1	5	0.045	4

*See note on n_{i1} and N_{i1} following Table 3-1.

Table 3-2. Temperature Calibration Error Sources, j = 1

In Table 3-2 note the use of the notation b_{i1}^- and b_{i1}^+. The superscripts minus and plus indicate the negative and positive bias limits.

When the bias limit is symmetrical, the ice reference junction bias would be reported as $\pm 0.1°F$. When some elemental bias limits are nonsymmetrical, the proper handling of the summations requires that all bias limits be defined as minus and plus limits. The ice reference junction bias limits, therefore, need to be noted as -0.1 to $+0.1°F$, as shown in Table 3-2.

Bias and precision error sources and their categories may be summarized as shown in Table 3-2.

Assuming the errors noted are the errors at the temperature calibration point of interest, the bias limits for the calibration are obtained as follows. Recalling Eq. (3-7):

$$B_1 = \pm [\Sigma (b_{i1})^2]^{1/2}$$

In this case, however, there are two levels of bias limits for each error source. These must be handled separately to produce a negative bias limit B^- and a positive limit B^+. These two limits are defined as:

$$B_1^- = \pm [\Sigma (b_{i1}^-)^2]^{1/2} \qquad (3\text{-}18)$$

and

$$B_1^+ = \pm [\Sigma (b_{i1}^+)^2]^{1/2} \qquad (3\text{-}19)$$

Eq. (3-18) and (3-19) are used separately to RSS the lower and upper bias limits. The calculation is:

$$B_1^- = -[(-0.7)^2 + (-0.1)^2 + (-0.2)^2]^{1/2}$$
$$= -0.73°F$$

and

$$B_1^+ = +[(+0.3)^2 + (+0.1)^2 + (+0.2)^2]^{1/2}$$
$$= +0.37°F$$

The bias limit for the experiment then has two parts and is stated as being from -0.73 to $+0.37\,°F$. Were there to be no precision errors, the true value, μ, would be contained in the uncertainty interval:

$$[\overline{X} - |B_1^+|] \le \mu \le [\overline{X} + |B_1^-|] \qquad (3\text{-}20)$$

CAREFULLY NOTE AN IMPORTANT EFFECT: A curious sign transformation has occurred in Eq. (3-20). The lower bias limit results in an error band above the average obtained, and the upper bias limit results in an error band below the average obtained. Carefully note the direction of the inequalities.

This can be more easily seen with actual data. For the case of zero precision error for the data in Table 3-2, using the results of the calculations of Equations (3-18) and (3-19) and recalling that the average calibration correction of interest is $2.00\,°F$, the uncertainty interval becomes:

$$[2.00 - |0.37|] \le \mu \le [2.00 + |-0.73|]$$
$$1.63\,°F \le \mu \le 2.73\,°F$$

Stated another way, the large negative bias limit, -0.73, will result in a test measurement being low. This means that the true value is above the average recorded. Similarly, a large positive bias limit, 0.37, will result in the true value being below the average recorded. This reasoning drives the use of the absolute value signs in the calculation of Eq. (3-20). Here, the true value is contained in the interval from 1.63 to $2.73\,°F$.

When bias limits are symmetrical, no such bookkeeping is necessary, as the choice of direction for the effect of the negative or positive bias limit is a wash.

The precision errors and combinations as well as the degrees of freedom are unaffected by the change to nonsymmetrical bias limits in the example.

3-7. Computing the Uncertainty Interval (Nonsymmetrical Bias Limits)

Even for nonsymmetrical bias limits, the measurement uncertainty is defined as the combination of both the systematic and random error components of error, bias, and precision. As before, two methods are available for that combination: U_{ADD} and U_{RSS}.

The Addition (ADD) Uncertainty Model (Nonsymmetrical Bias Limits)

The information is now available to compute the uncertainty interval, or measurement uncertainty, for the case in Table 3-2 with nonsymmetrical bias limits. Here, the notation of U_{ADD}^- and U_{ADD}^+ will be used to denote the lower and upper limits of the nonsymmetrical uncertainty statement.

$$U_{ADD}^- = [B^- - t_{95}S] \qquad (3-21)$$

$$U_{ADD}^+ = [B^+ + t_{95}S] \qquad (3-22)$$

This states that the uncertainty is from U_{ADD}^- to U_{ADD}^+. For the data in Table 3-2 this is:

$$U_{ADD}^- = [-0.73 - (2.080 \times 0.073)] = -0.88$$

and

$$U_{ADD}^+ = [0.37 + (2.080 \times 0.073)] = 0.52°F$$

The true value is contained in the interval:

$$(\overline{X} - |U_{ADD}^+|) \le \mu \le (\overline{X} + |U_{ADD}^-|) \qquad (3-23)$$

Recalling that the calibration average correction was $2.00°F$ at the temperature of interest, the data can be filled into Equation (3-23) to obtain:

$$(2.00 - |0.52|) \le \mu \le (2.00 + |-0.88|)$$

$$1.48°F \le \mu \le 2.88°F$$

See Fig. 3-3 for an illustration of the error bounds. This figure illustrates the effect of the nonsymmetrical bias limits on the uncertainty derived from the data in Table 3-2.

Here, as with the pure bias case above, the lower limit for the uncertainty, U_{ADD}^- results in an error band *above* the average correction obtained. This is because the lower uncertainty limit results in a reading below the true value. Similarly, the upper uncertainty limit results in an error band *below* the average obtained.

The Root-Sum-Square Uncertainty Interval (Nonsymmetrical Bias Limits)

Similar results may be obtained for the RSS uncertainty model. The U_{RSS}^- and U_{RSS}^+ calculations are left as an exercise for the student (see Exercise 3-6).

Error Category	Systematic (Bias Limit)	Random (Precision Index)	Degrees of Freedom
1	b_{11} $\left.\begin{array}{}\\ \\ \end{array}\right\}$ b_{21} $RSS = B_1$ b_{31}	$s_{11}/\sqrt{N_{11}} = S_{11}$ $s_{21}/\sqrt{N_{21}} = S_{21}$ $RSS = S_1$ $s_{31}/\sqrt{N_{31}} = S_{31}$	ν_{11} ν_{21} $W/S = \nu_1$ ν_{31}
2	b_{12} b_{22} $RSS = B_2$ b_{32}	$s_{12}/\sqrt{N_{12}} = S_{12}$ $s_{22}/\sqrt{N_{22}} = S_{22}$ $RSS = S_2$ $s_{32}/\sqrt{N_{32}} = S_{32}$	ν_{12} ν_{22} $W/S = \nu_2$ ν_{32}
3	b_{13} b_{23} $RSS = B_3$ b_{33}	$s_{13}/\sqrt{N_{13}} = S_{13}$ $s_{23}/\sqrt{N_{23}} = S_{23}$ $RSS = S_3$ $s_{33}/\sqrt{N_{33}} = S_{33}$	ν_{13} ν_{23} $W/S = \nu_3$ ν_{33}
	↓ RSS = B, the systematic error component of the uncertainty	↓ RSS = S, the precision index of the result	↓ $W/S = \nu$, the degrees of freedom of S

Note: Only RSS errors with the same units. Propagate errors into result units before combining with RSS.

W/S = the Welch–Satterswaithe method for combining degrees of freedom. As with RSS, all the S's must have the same units.

RSS = the root-sum-square

Error Category	Bias Limit	Precision Index	Degrees of Freedom	≈ Precision of Source
1	B_1	S_1	ν_1	$t_{95}S_1$
2	B_2	S_2	ν_2	$t_{95}S_2$
3	B_3	S_3	ν_3	$t_{95}S_3$
	↓ RSS = B	↓ RSS = S	↓ $W/S = \nu$	

$$U_{ADD} = \pm [B + t_{95}S]$$

$$U_{RSS} = \pm [B^2 + (t_{95}S)^2]^{1/2}$$

Note: B = the bias limit of the result
  S = the precision index of the result
  ν = the degrees of freedom of S
  t_{95} = the Student's t for degrees of freedom
  $t_{95}S$ = the random error component of the uncertainty

Table 3-3. Uncertainty Summary for Three Error Categories with Three Elemental Error Sources Each

3-8. Most Common Uncertainty Model Summary

By far the most common uncertainty model is summarized in Table 3-3 for the case of three categories and three error sources in each category. Table 3-3 shows clearly the summation and handling of the degrees of freedom. It can be used as a guide for as many categories as needed, with as many as possible error sources in each category. Table 3-3 is the uncertainty calculation for a single measurement or the measurement of a single parameter such as temperature.

If the result is not a simple parameter measurement such as temperature or pressure, Table 3-3 is used for each parameter measurement used to calculate a result; that is, for example, B, S, and ν would be calculated for temperature, pressure, etc., and those values propagated into the final result uncertainty. This error propagation is covered in Unit 5.

If only the uncertainty of a single measurement result, e.g., temperature, is needed, the uncertainty is as shown in Table 3-3. To go further and determine the uncertainty for several measurements, the random error component of the uncertainty would again be divided by the square root of the number of measurements, M; That is, for multiple measurements:

$t_{95}S/\sqrt{M}$ = the random error component of the uncertainty
for several, M, measurements of one parameter
such as temperature or pressure

M = the number of measurements to be averaged
for a parameter

3-9. Summary

In this unit the basics of the error categorization process and the uncertainty statement have been presented. It is now possible for the student to calculate the measurement uncertainty for simple measurement systems.

References

1. ANSI/ASME PTC 19.1-1985, *Performance Test Code, Instruments and Apparatus, Part 1, Measurement Uncertainty*, p. 7.
2. Bowker, A. H., and Lieberman, E. H., *Experimental Statistics*, p. 99-1-1, Prentice-Hall (1969).
3. Op cit., *Performance Test Code*, p. 12.

4. Coleman, H. W., and Steele, Jr., W. G., *Experimentation and Uncertainty Analysis for Engineers*, p. 97, John Wiley & Sons (1989).
5. Brownlee, K. A., *Statistical Theory and Methodology in Science and Engineering*, second edition, p. 300, John Wiley & Sons (1967).
6. Abernethy, R. B., and Ringhiser, B., *The History and Statistical Development of the New ASME-SAE-AIAA-ISO Measurement Uncertainty Methodology*, AIAA/SAE/ASME/ASEE 21st Joint Propulsion Conference, Monterey, CA, July 8–10, 1985.
7. Abernethy, R. B., et al., *Handbook—Gas Turbine Measurement Uncertainty*, AEDC (1973).

Exercises:

3-1. *Bias Limit Problem*

Consider the following list of bias limits: 1, 2, 3, 10.
   a. *What would you get after combining them to obtain the bias of the test result?*
       1) 10.68   2) 106.00   3) 13.74   4) _____
   b. *Same as (a) but with bias limits of: 1, 2, 3, 10, 11, 12.*
       1) 19.47   2) 39.00   3) 36.74   4) _____
   c. *What is learned about the impact of large errors?*

3-2. *Precision Index Problems*

Consider the following precision indexes for two error sources:

$$S_1 = 1.0\% \qquad \nu_1 = 10 \text{ degrees of freedom}$$
$$S_2 = 2.0\% \qquad \nu_2 = 20 \text{ degrees of freedom}$$

   a. *What is the precision index of the combination $S = (S_1^2 + S_2^2)^{1/2}$?*
   b. *What are the equivalent degrees of freedom? (Note: Use the Welch-Satterthwaite approximation.)*
   c. What is $t_{95} * S$? (This is the random error component of the uncertainty.)

3-3. Combining Degrees of Freedom Problem

Write the formula for the S_j's.

3-4. *Truncating Degrees of Freedom Problem*

Why is truncating the fractional degrees of freedom obtained with the Welch-Satterthwaite approximation conservative?

3-5. Root-Sum-Square Uncertainty Interval Problem

Write the formulas for U_{RSS}^- and U_{RSS}^+ and determine the numerical values for the example in Section 3-7.

3-6. Scale and Truth Problem

Consider every possible error source for a measurement process that consists of daily weighings on your bathroom scale in preparation for your annual physical examination when you will be weighed on your doctor's scale. Categorize the errors into bias and precision.
   a. What is truth in this process?
   b. How would you calibrate your scale?
   c. How would you estimate the precision index?
   d. Make your best estimate of the bias limit and precision index of a typical bathroom scale.

Unit 4:
How to Do It Summary

UNIT 4

How to Do It Summary

In this unit the nomenclature will be explained, there will be emphasis on specific steps used in an uncertainty analysis, and details will be presented on how to estimate both precision errors and bias limits. Step by step instructions along with the treatment of calibration errors and the timing of an uncertainty analysis will also be considered. This unit will reinforce the fundamentals of the statistics and data analysis needed to complete a credible measurement uncertainty analysis.

Learning Objectives — When you have completed this unit, you should:

    A. Understand and be able to compute precision indexes and bias limits.

    B. Be able to properly combine precision indexes and bias limits.

    C. Understand the proper treatment of calibration errors.

    D. Understand the need for and be able to complete both pretest and posttest uncertainty analyses.

    E. Understand the statistical basis for uncertainty analysis.

While some of the methods presented in this unit are covered in parts of other units, it is sometimes easier for the student to have a central reference for this material. Hence, this information is presented in readable format.

4-1. Review of Nomenclature

The nomenclature used thus far has covered S_X, $S_{\overline{X}}$, X, $\overline{X}$, n, N, B, t_{95}, and U. These are the generic parameters whose definitions may be summarized as follows:

    S_X = the standard deviation of a data set or sample, sometimes shown as s

    $S_{\overline{X}}$ = the standard deviation of the sample average, also called the precision index, sometimes shown as S

X = the individual data point, sometimes called X_i
$\overline{X}$ = the average of the data set or sample of X_i's
n = the number of data points used to calculate S_X
N = the number of data points in the average $\overline{X}$
B = the bias or systematic error component of the uncertainty
t_{95} = the Student's t statistic at 95% confidence
U = the uncertainty of an experiment or measurement

All the above are nomenclature and symbols used to describe a data set or sample and an error in a data set. Except for N and t_{95}, none of them are exact. They all are estimates of the true value of the population and are obtained from the sample of data taken. Note that for simple situations, usually N = n.

The population true values are:

σ_X = the standard deviation of the population
$\sigma_{\overline{X}}$ = the standard deviation of a set of averages taken from the population
ϵ = the actual random error of a data point; it is a value never known
β = the true bias error for a data point or set of data; it is a value never known
$\delta = \epsilon + \beta$; the true total error or uncertainty of a data point; it is a value never known

The above true values are never known but may only be estimated, using the variables mentioned above. This is summarized in Table 4-1. As can be seen, an experimenter or measurement specialist never knows the true values for errors. Only estimates are known, as drawn from the sample of data taken. The following material, therefore, concentrates on sample statistics and the statistical basis for the calculation of uncertainty.

Error Type	True Error	Uncertainty (Limit)
Random	ϵ	$t_{95}S_X/\sqrt{N}$ or $t_{95}\,S_{\overline{X}}$
Systematic	β	B
Total	$\delta = \epsilon + \beta$	U_{ADD} or U_{RSS}

Table 4-1. Comparison of Population and Sample Statistics [The true error compared with the estimate of the true error, the uncertainty (limit).]

4-2. How To Do It Summary

Now that the reader has been introduced to the basics, this
section will present an outline of the techniques used to obtain
an uncertainty analysis. There are seven parts to this approach:

A. Calculation of precision indexes

B. Obtaining and combining bias limits

C. How to do it summary

D. Treatment of calibration errors

E. Making pretest estimates of uncertainty and why

F. Making posttest estimates of uncertainty and why

4-3. Calculation of Precision Indexes

In this section, several ways to obtain the precision index will
be presented. All are based on the standard deviation of the
data, S_X.

$$S_X = [\Sigma(X_i - \overline{X})^2/(n - 1)]^{1/2} \qquad (4\text{-}1)$$

The standard deviation of the data is calculated with Eq. (4-1).
It is not the precision index. The precision index is calculated
using Eq. (3-2). Generically, that equation is:

$$S_{\overline{X}} = S_X/\sqrt{N} \qquad (4\text{-}2)$$

Remember that the precision index is the estimate of the
standard deviation of the average. It is an estimate of the
standard deviation of a group of averages from samples of data
with the same number of data points as the sample taken to
yield the $S_{\overline{X}}$ already obtained from the data.

The key then is to first obtain the standard deviation of the
data. There are at least four ways to do that:

A. When the variable being measured can be held constant
   and "n" repeats

B. When there are "m" redundant measurements each with "n" repeats

C. When there is a pair of redundant measurements of the same variable at the same time

D. When there is applicable calibration data

Calculating S_X When the Variable Being Measured Can Be Held Constant

When the measured variable can be held constant, the standard deviation of the data can be used to calculate the precision index of the measurement system by utilizing Eq. (4-2). This is the simplest and the most common case. After a test, for example, the variability in the data may be expressed as S_X. The precision index follows immediately. The precision index is the expected scatter, were repeat averages possible to obtain.

Calculating S_X When There Are "m" Redundant Measurements Each with "n" Repeats

This is a special case of a more common method called pooling. The general expression for S_X when there are "m" redundant measurements with "n" repeats is:

$$S_X = \{\Sigma\Sigma(X_{ik} - \overline{X}_k)^2/[(m \times n) - m]\}^{1/2} \qquad (4\text{-}3)$$

Here, the double sum is first over k and then over i.

Eq. (4-3) is actually a special case when all m groups of data have the same number of data points, n. The general formula for pooling is:

$$S_X = S_{pooled} = \left(\frac{\nu_1 S_1^2 + \nu_2 S_2^2 + \cdots + \nu_m S_m^2}{\nu_1 + \nu_2 + \cdots + \nu_m}\right)^{1/2} \qquad (4\text{-}4)$$

It is recommended that Eq. (4-4) be utilized all the time. It never fails.

Pooling data from several sets or samples, as is done in Eq. (4-4), provides a better estimate of the standard deviation of the population of data than any one sample can provide.

Again, once the standard deviation of the data is obtained, the precision index follows easily. Just divide the resulting S_X by the number of data points averaged to get $\overline{X}$. Note again, that the N used is related to the number of data points averaged, not the number of data points or the degrees of freedom in the various samples.

The degrees of freedom for Eq. (4-4) constitute the sum of the degrees of freedom for all the m samples. It is the defining parameter used to obtain t_{95} in an uncertainty analysis. It is needed to obtain the random error component of the uncertainty, $t_{95}S_{\overline{X}}$.

Calculating S_X When There Is a Pair of Redundant Measurements of the Same Variable at the Same Time

It is often not realized that instrument or measurement system precision may be estimated with no knowledge of the measurement system or variable being measured except for: (1) the assumption that two identical instruments or measurement systems have the same precision and (2) the assumption that the variable being measured is the same for both instruments or systems. For example, if it is desired to estimate the precision of two CO_2 analyzers, it can be done without knowing the level of CO_2 being measured. All that is needed is to assume that the instruments respond identically and that both instruments see the same process stream.

In this case, the test data is analyzed to determine the standard deviation of the deltas between the instruments, S_Δ, which is defined by Eq. (4-5):

$$S_\Delta = [\Sigma(\Delta_i - \overline{\Delta})^2/(n-1)]^{1/2} \qquad (4\text{-}5)$$

Eq. (4-5) is just the standard deviation of a set of data where all the i data points are deltas.

It is important to note then that S_Δ is related to the standard deviation of either the instruments or measurement systems. They are related by Eq. (4-6):

$$S_X = S_\Delta/\sqrt{2} \qquad (4\text{-}6)$$

The proof for this equation will be an exercise for the student in Unit 5.

It can be seen, therefore, that as long as an instrument and/or a measurement system see the same variable at the same time and as long as they have the same precision, the standard deviation for the data from either may be estimated with Eqs. (4-5) and (4-6).

The precision index, $S_{\bar{X}}$, is then obtained using Eq. (4-7):

$$S_{\bar{X}} = S_X/\sqrt{N}$$
$$= S_\Delta/(\sqrt{2N}) \qquad (4\text{-}7)$$

Eq. (4-7) will prove to be a valuable tool when simultaneous measurements from two instruments are available. It is used after a test is run and the delta data is obtained. N is the number of test data points that will be averaged into a test result. Yes, the precision index depends not only on the standard deviation of the data but also on the number of data points to be averaged.

Here, the degrees of freedom associated with $S_{\bar{X}}$ is one less than the number of data points used to calculate S_Δ.

Calculating S_X When There Is Applicable Calibration Data

Another method for estimating the precision index of an instrument is to use calibration data. This is effective only when the calibration process may be deemed to yield instrument performance identical to that obtained on the process stream.

That one constraint on instrument performance may be ascertained from calibration data taken in the field or on the test site itself with a portable standard. This will work as long as the standard has a precision that is significantly lower than the test instrument. In this way all the precision evident in the on-site calibration may be attributed to the measurement instrument or system and not to the standard.

In this case, the precision index is obtained simply from the standard deviation of the calibration data. It is important to realize here that it is assumed that only one level is being calibrated in this discussion. For the proper treatment of more than one level or calibration constant, called a calibration curve or line, see Section 7-4.

Once the standard deviation of the calibration data is obtained, one merely divides it by the square root of N, the number of test data points that will be averaged into a test result. This is shown in Eq. (4-8).

$$S_{\overline{X}} = S_{CAL}/\sqrt{N} \tag{4-8}$$

Remember here that S_{CAL} is the standard deviation of the calibration data for a single calibration constant. N is the number of test data points that will be averaged into the test result. Here, too, the degrees of freedom for $S_{\overline{X}}$ are the same as that for S_{CAL}.

4-4. Obtaining and Combining Bias Limits

Obtaining Bias Limits

It is possible that the most difficult part of any uncertainty analysis is the obtaining of bias limits. Frequently, there is no data from which to calculate a bias limit or bias estimate.

Reference 1 recommends five possible ways to to obtain bias limits:

    A. Interlaboratory comparisons

    B. Standards in the test environment

    C. Auxiliary or concomitant functions

    D. Bias from special causes, special tests

    E. Judgment or estimation

The above are in rough order of preference to the experimenter. The first is by far the best as it has a solid basis in data. The last is by far the worst, relying on judgment alone with all its foibles.

Interlaboratory Comparisons

Almost all experimenters or metrologists agree that the best way to get a handle on their own facility's bias limit is to run interfacility comparisons or tests. These tests, often called round robins, require a stable set of standards or measurement artifacts that may be sent from one place to another without affecting its average value or precision. Each facility in turn then measures this artifact and the results from all the facilities are analyzed, usually by an independent analyst; it is also usually the case that the analyst does not know which test result is from which participating facility or laboratory.

The results from this kind of series of tests may be taken two ways. First, the variability observed between laboratories, S_{IL} (standard deviation interlaboratory), may be used to estimate the precision across laboratories. That is, approximately 95% of the results from various laboratories will be contained in the interval $\overline{X} \pm t_{95}S_{IL}$. It is then used as an estimate of the bias for any one laboratory, $t_{95}S_{IL}$.

Standards in the Test Environment

Sometimes it is possible to take a mobile standard out to the test environment and calibrate the measurement system in place. This method of calibration is similar to the National Institute of Standards and Technology's (NIST) Measurement Assurance Program (MAP).

In this method of bias estimation, a carefully documented, stable set of calibration artifacts are sent to the calibration laboratory for calibration. There is a significant difference from a normal calibration, however. In the normal case, an instrument or measurement system is calibrated by comparing it to a standard, usually more accurate than the instrument under calibration, in order to determine a calibration constant or calibration curve for the instrument. In this application, the standard is assumed to be more accurate than the instrument, and the correction or calibration curve is then used to correct test data to be more closely aligned with the standard.

The calibration process is assumed to have very small or no bias errors, and the precision of the data may be used to assess the random error component of the measurement uncertainty. However, it is known that every measurement process has bias or systematic error. The standard instrument may be calibrated, but the process in which it is used in the laboratory cannot be calibrated by normal means. This is the strength of the MAP. The carefully monitored portable standards are sent to the calibration laboratory and calibrated as though they are test instruments. The big difference is that the errors observed are attributed to the calibration process and the laboratory standard, not to the "instrument" or calibration artifact being calibrated.

By calibrating a standard in the laboratory, the errors in the process itself may be identified and quantified. Such is the case in any test when a standard may be used to calibrate the instruments or measurement systems at the test site. The errors observed may be used to assess the bias errors of the measurement process itself. The standard is assumed correct, except for its document bias errors. The process itself— instrument, standards and methods—are presumed to account for the remaining differences observed. The differences observed may be used to estimate the bias of the measurement process.

Auxiliary or Concomitant Functions

It is sometimes the case that bias error for several independent methods may be estimated by comparing the test results obtained when using all the methods on the same process stream. It is important that the measurement methods be independent; that is, their error sources have no relationship from one method to another. These independent methods are sometimes called concomitant methods.

As an example, air flow in a gas turbine test may be determined by an orifice in the inlet duct, an inlet bellmouth (nozzle) on the engine, a compressor speed-flow map, the turbine flow parameter, and the exhaust nozzle coefficient. Each of these measurements may be set up to be independent. The degree of disagreement between them may be used to estimate the bias typical of any. That is, assuming each has the same bias, the scatter between the air flow measured may be used to estimate a single bias limit magnitude assignable to any of them.

Example 4-1:
It may be assumed that the values for gas turbine air flows obtained by the five methods might be as follows:

Measurement Method	Value Obtained
Pipe orifice	230.1 lbs/sec
Inlet bellmouth	224.7 lbs/sec
Compressor map	245.8 lbs/sec
Turbine flow parameter	232.4 lbs/sec
Nozzle coefficient	228.7 lbs/sec

For the above data, $\overline{X} = 232.3$ and $S_X = 8.0$. The bias limit assignable to each of the above methods is $t_{95}S_X$. t_{95} is obtained from Appendix D for four (4) degrees of freedom (one less than the number of methods being utilized in this calculation). t_{95} equals 2.776, so the bias limit is estimated as $2.776 \times 8.0 = 22.2$ lbs/sec. This means that the estimate of the bias limit is 22.2 lbs/sec for each of the concomitant methods. (Removing known precision error as well is considered in Unit 7.)

Bias from Special Causes, Special Tests

Special tests can always be designed to evaluate the systematic errors that may exist in a measurement process. Special calibrations may be run to perturb the parameter of interest throughout its range, thus revealing potential bias error sources and estimates of the bias limits. Usually, the experimenter will be the best person to suggest ways to evaluate what the bias limit might be.

Judgment or Estimation

By far the worst method for estimating the magnitude of a bias limit is judgment. When there is no data or the process is so unique that special calibrations or tests are not available, the judgment of the engineer, experimenter, or researcher must be used.

Here, the problem is pride. Many experimenters will not admit that their experiment or measurement system has any likelihood of any error, let alone the possibility that significant systematic error occurs that would displace all their measurements from the true value. Often the experimenter will point to low precision errors and assume there is no bias to speak of. This must be countered with the argument that some bias always exists and must be estimated.

It should also be noted that the truly competent experimenter does have a good idea of the magnitude of the measurement system errors. What is needed is to get him or her to reveal true feelings about their magnitude.

Throughout, however, this remains the worst method for bias limit estimation. It often yields unreasonably small errors and

always yields bias limits that are difficult to defend to a third
party.

Avoid this method at all costs!

Combining Bias Limits

There are three major methods in the current literature for
combining bias limits. Only one is recommended and has
legitimacy from an established standard. These three methods
follow, with the least acceptable first and the recommended one
last.

Summing Bias Limits

The simplest method for combining bias limits is to simply
sum them. Eq. (4-9) illustrates the mathematics of this simplest
approach.

$$B = \pm[\Sigma\Sigma(b_{ij})] \tag{4-9}$$

As has been usual, the double sum is over the number of error
sources, i, in error categories, j.

This method is heartily not recommended, as it yields a bias
limit much too large to be reasonable. Consider, for example,
the following three elemental bias limits where there is only
one category:

$$b_{11} = \pm5.0°F$$
$$b_{21} = \pm7.3°F$$
$$b_{31} = \pm4.5°F$$

Using Eq. (4-9), the bias limit would be:

$$B = \pm(5.0 + 7.3 + 4.5)°F$$
$$= \pm16.8°F$$

This limit has meaning. If, for example, the elemental bias
limits represent 95% confidence estimates of error, then having
an estimate of their combined effect of 16.8 means that the
individual elemental errors have high probability of each being
at their extreme limit, or upper 97.5/lower 2.5 percentile. For
the first elemental bias limit, there is one chance in 20 that it

will be at one or the other extreme. There is one chance in 40 that it will be high and one in 40 that it would be low. The same is true for the second and third. For all three to be at their same either upper or lower extremes, the condition modeled by summing the bias limits, the odds are $(1/40)^3$, or 1 in 64,000! This is extremely unlikely and much poorer odds than the recommended bias limit coverage of about 1 in 20 chances of the true bias being outside the quoted limits.

The use of this method is obviously unreasonable.

Summing Major Elemental Bias Limits and Root-Sum-Squaring Minor Ones

In the second method, summing major elemental bias limits and root-sum-squaring minor ones, the square root is taken of the square of the sum of the three or four largest elemental bias limits combined with the sum of the squares of the rest. Eq. (4-10) expresses this model.

$$B = \pm[\{\Sigma\Sigma[(\text{largest})b_{ij}]\}^2 + [\Sigma\Sigma(b_{ij})^2]]^{1/2} \qquad (4\text{-}10)$$

This is also an unreasonable approach, which can be understood by examining Example 4-2.

Example 4-2:
Consider the three elemental bias limits of category 1 presented previously, and add to them the following three from category 2:

$$b_{12} = \pm 0.2°F$$
$$b_{22} = \pm 0.1°F$$
$$b_{32} = \pm 0.3°F$$

With this approach, the first three elemental bias limits from category 1 would be summed to yield $B_1 = \pm 16.8°F$ as before; the sum of the squares of the last three from category 2 would yield B_2 as follows:

$$(B_2)^2 = \pm(0.2^2 + 0.1^2 + 0.3^2)$$
$$= (\pm 0.14°F)$$

Combining these two terms into Eq. (4-10), the following is obtained:

$$B = \pm[(16.8)^2 + 0.14]^{1/2}$$
$$= \pm 16.8°F$$

This result is as unreasonable as the first model's. The additional terms obtained from the three small errors are lost completely in the impact of the sum of the largest three. This, too, is an extremely unlikely result for a bias limit.

Root-Sum-Square of the Elemental Bias Limits

The recommended method is to root-sum-square the elemental bias limits. Its calculation is expressed by Eq. (3-7):

$$B = \pm[\Sigma\Sigma(b_{ij})^2]^{1/2}$$

Its application was illustrated in the previous unit but will be reviewed here.

Consider the first three elemental bias limits above. For them,

$$B = \pm[5.0^2 + 7.3^2 + 4.5^2]^{1/2}$$
$$= \pm[9.9°F]$$

This result is reasonable as it allows for the distinct possibility that some elemental bias errors (their limits are merely expressions of their possible range) will be positive and others negative, thus having the effect of partial cancellation; hence, this result, which is more than the largest bias limit (expected) but much less than the linear sum, which is so unlikely. Had all these elemental bias limits been 95% coverage, the result too would also have been 95% coverage, or one chance in 20 that the actual bias error would be greater than the plus or minus limit shown.

Were the calculation to include the small limits, they would have little effect even in this model. This is left as an exercise for the student.

Summary

The recommended combination method for bias limits then is the root-sum-square approach, as recommended by the ASME standard, Reference 2.

4-5. Nonsymmetrical Bias Limits

In all the preceding discussion, the assumption was made that the bias limits were symmetrical. That is, they were plus or minus the same absolute amount. Although this is not always the case, the recommended approach to their combination does not change when it isn't. What is affected is the impact on the uncertainty band for the systematic error portion of the uncertainty, the bias.

As is the case of a symmetrical bias limit, the true value for the measurement or experiment likely lies within the distance from the average and the average plus or minus the bias limit. However, what is missed in this argument is that the true value is in the range of the average plus the negative bias limit and the range of the average minus the positive bias limit. A negative bias limit means the measurement is below the true value. A positive bias limit means the measurement is above the true value.

This distinction is completely lost for symmetrical bias limits and no one cares. However, for nonsymmetrical bias limits, the effect is striking. Fig. 4-1 illustrates this effect for the case in

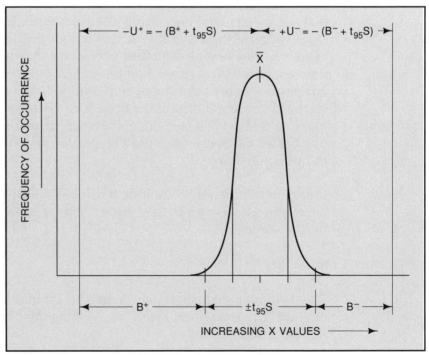

Fig. 4-1. U_{ADD} **Nonsymmetrical Uncertainty Interval**

which there is significant precision error. It is easier to understand when the precision error is zero and will be explained as such here for clarity and reinforcement.

Suppose the final bias limit is nonsymmetrical and is expressed as:

$$B^- = -5.0°F$$
$$B^+ = +2.0°F$$

In the case in which there is no precision error, the true value is in the range of $(\overline{X} + |B^-|)$ down to $(\overline{X} - |B^+|)$, or, $(\overline{X} + 5.0°F)$ down to $(\overline{X} - 2.0°F)$.

In this case, the effect of the bias limit is the reverse of the expected. It is illustrated in Figure 4-1.

As shown in Unit 3, nonsymmetrical bias limits lead to nonsymmetrical uncertainty intervals.

4-6. Step-by-Step Instructions

Although this ILM is not intended to be a cook book for uncertainty analysis, some specific steps should be taken when embarking on such an analysis. These generalized steps are outlined in Reference 3 and described below.

Step 1. Define the measurement system.

The purpose of this step is to consider all aspects of the test situation: the calibrations, the duration, the instruments, the data acquisition, the error propagation (covered in Unit 5), the data reduction, and the presentation of results (covered in Unit 8). The test objective should be clearly stated, including the success criteria; that is, state what level of what parameter must be achieved to declare the test or experiment a success. DO NOT ALLOW YOURSELF TO JUST RUN THE TEST OR EXPERIMENT. CONSIDER THE RESULTS AND THEN DECIDE UPON THE SUCCESS OR FAILURE OF THE NEW PROCESS. Do this honestly and do it before the test.

Include in that assessment of success criteria what uncertainty is acceptable. Go into an experiment or test with a result goal that includes a maximum permissible measurement uncertainty. Note that it may be necessary here to carefully define the performance or calculation equations to do this right.

This process, then, is usually done before a test. It is only then that this approach is needed to define the precision errors. After a test is run, the data itself will usually be sufficiently voluminous to permit a direct calculation of precision error from the test results. This process should still be applied, even posttest, to obtain the bias limit.

Step by step, this part of the process includes the following:

A. List all the independent parameters and their expected levels.

B. List all required calibrations and how the data is to be reduced.

C. List and define all the data reduction calculations required to obtain the test result from the measurement parameters.

Step 2. List all the error sources.

The intent is to compile a complete, exhaustive list of all possible error sources, bias and precision, without regard to a consideration of their possible size or impact on the experimental result.

Step by step, this part of the process is as follows:

A. List all the error sources.

B. If convenient, group the error sources into calibration, data acquisition, data reduction, and errors of method categories. This step is not a necessity for a viable uncertainty analysis, but it often makes the analysis itself easier and clearer.

C. Further group the error sources into bias and precision errors. Here, a simple rule will help: *if the error source will cause scatter in your test result, it is a precision error; if not, it is a bias.* This rule will never fail and should be used with confidence.

Step 3. Estimate the magnitude of all the elemental error sources.

Here, the precision errors may be estimated from previous test data or inferred from calibration data. The bias errors should be obtained in one of the five suggested ways discussed earlier in this unit under "Obtaining Bias Limits."

Step 4. Calculate the bias and precision errors for each parameter in the test.

Combine bias and precision elemental errors to obtain the bias limit and the precision index for each parameter measured in the experiment or test. The methods of Unit 3 should be used for this combination of errors.

Step 5. Propagate the bias limit and the precision index into the test result using the methods of Unit 5.

It is important to remember to ascertain whether the errors being combined are independent or not. The methods of Unit 3 are only for independent error sources and, happily, most measurement parameters are. However, when the same error source shows up in several places in a test result, the error sources are not independent. The propagation formulas that are designed for that situation must be used. Those also are given in Unit 5.

Step 6. Calculate the uncertainty.

The second-to-last step is to calculate the uncertainty. This is merely the sum of the bias limit and the precision index for the test result. The sum will be linear addition for the U_{ADD} and root-sum-square for the U_{RSS} model.

Step 7. Report the uncertainty.

When reporting the test or experimental result uncertainty, it is important also to independently report the bias limit, the precision index, and the degrees of freedom that are associated with the latter. It is important to also report the uncertainty model used; that is, the U_{ADD} or U_{RSS}. Unit 8 provides a detailed treatment of the reporting of measurement uncertainty.

4-7. Treatment of Calibration Errors

When considering the steps to an uncertainty analysis, it is important to carefully examine the calibration errors. Single calibrations, multiple calibrations, and back-to-back tests all utilize calibration data—the same calibration data—differently.

Single Calibration, Short Test

In this application, the test or experiment is run over a time interval that is short. In this case, all the calibration errors manifest themselves only once, in the single calibration constant or curve. This constant or curve never changes for the duration of the experiment. This is the definition of a short test: the calibration constant or curve never changes.

Here, in spite of the fact that both bias and precision errors contribute to the uncertainty of the calibration, all the error of the calibration results in a bias for the rest of the experiment. Not even the precision errors in the calibration process contribute to scatter in the test result.

It may be thought of this way: If the calibration constant or curve never changes for the experiment, whatever error has displaced it from its true value also does not change for the duration of the experiment. It is a constant, or systematic error, bias. The actual magnitude of this error is not known—only its limits. The proper expression of the limits of this kind of calibration error is called fossilized error; that is, all the error of the calibration process is fossilized into bias for the test or experiment. The equation to be used is:

$$B_{CAL} = [B^2 + (t_{95}S_{\overline{X}})^2]^{1/2} \qquad (4\text{-}11)$$

Here, all the error of the calibration process has been fossilized into a bias term for the rest of the calibration hierarchy. Eq. (4-11) is in generic form. The actual bias limits and precision indexes so utilized are the combination of all the elemental error sources in the calibration process.

Note that this fossilization process often should occur more than once. It occurs at every level in the measurement hierarchy where a constant, average, or calibration curve is calculated and remains unchanged for the rest of the measurement hierarchy below it.

Many Calibrations, Long Test

When there is a long test with many calibrations, the errors in the calibration process will contribute scatter in the long-term test results. This is because there will be many calibrations throughout the test process. In this case, the usual root-sum-square of elemental bias errors and precision indexes is done as shown in Unit 3 for the calibration error sources along with the other error sources.

Here the calibration errors are combined into the systematic and random portions of the uncertainty right along with the other error sources. The applicable equations are the standard:

$$B_{CAL} = [\Sigma(b_i)^2] \qquad (4\text{-}12)$$
$$t_{95}S_{CAL} = t[\Sigma(S_i)^2]^{1/2} \qquad (4\text{-}13)$$

In both Eqs. (4-12) and (4-13), only calibration errors are considered and only for that one category; that is, j, the category, is assumed to be 1 and is not shown for clarity.

Zero Calibration Errors, Back-to-Back Tests

One very effective way to see clearly a small effect in test results is to employ the technique called back-to-back testing. In this case, a test or experiment is run, and then, rapidly, a change in the test object is made and the test is repeated. The time here must be short, and no recalibration of the measurement system between tests is allowed.

The test must be short enough so that it can be assumed that no instrument or measurement system drift or decalibration occurs. In addition, no recalibration of the instruments or measurement system may occur or the calibration constant or curve will shift. This will violate a fundamental principle of back-to-back testing; that is, the bias errors of the calibration process do not have time or opportunity to shift between the two tests. If this is true and the test time is short, all the calibration error is bias, as explained above. In addition, *all the calibration error is zero!* This rather surprising result occurs because the same bias or systematic error that affects the first test also affects the second. Since back-to-back tests are designed to measure differences, not absolute levels, any bias error in the calibration will not affect the difference and is zero by definition.

If the first test is high by 10 psi, the second test will be also, and the difference in psi will be unaffected by the bias error from calibrations.

This technique should be employed whenever small changes need to be observed in large parameters.

4-8. The Timing of an Uncertainty Analysis

There are two major times an uncertainty analysis should be done. One is pretest, or before a test is even run. The other is posttest, or after the test results are in for analysis. Pretest uncertainty analysis tells the experimenter whether or not the planned test is adequate to observe the effect of interest. Posttest uncertainty analysis provides a diagnostic test that reveals the value of the data for decision making.

Pretest Uncertainty Estimates

To the uninitiated experimenter, the first response to the suggestion that a pretest uncertainty analysis is needed is, "Why bother?" What is often missed is that every experimenter does an uncertainty analysis. It is usually after the test and suggests that either the uncertainty is low (results match predictions) or that it is large (results refute predictions). Neither of these approaches to uncertainty analysis is appropriate.

A pretest uncertainty analysis is a test planning tool that, when done correctly, yields two major kinds of information:

A. Is the experiment worth running? Will the expected test result be observable considering the testing errors?

B. If the uncertainty is too large, what should be done to reduce the error so that the test result might be observable with confidence?

It is foolishness to design a test to demonstrate a 0.5 percent improvement in compressor efficiency, for example, and then use a measurement system that has an uncertainty of $\pm 1.0\%$. Any test result observed has a high likelihood of having been caused by the errors of the measurement system and not the design change intended to improve the compressor efficiency. Therefore, the primary question to be answered by a pretest uncertainty analysis is: *Is the predicted accuracy good enough?* Or, is the test result clearly observable in the fog of the measurement errors?

Numerous responses are received from an experimenter, who is low on budget and who realizes that an uncertainty analysis may be appropriate but may not want to admit it. Such experimenters fall into five categories.

A. Ostrich—"I don't want you guys putting fuzz bands on my data." The fallacy here is that the "fuzz bands" are already there and all that an uncertainty analysis will do is make them visible and addressable. Ignoring them, like the ostrich, will only yield major problems down the road.

B. Doubter—"I don't believe in all that uncertainty mumbo jumbo." This type of individual needs an education. Uncertainty analysis is a simple approach to putting objective limits on the validity of data. It contributes to an understanding of the test result.

C. Indifferent—"This is not my favorite subject." This experimenter is more worried about conducting the test than about what value may be realized from the data. It is important to understand that the data has value only if the effects being searched for exceed the uncertainty. It should be every experimenter's "favorite subject."

D. Converted—"After talking to you guys, I get the impression that if I don't start worrying about validity I'm going straight to hell." This individual has seen that validity, or uncertainty analysis, is critical to a successful test program.

E. Biblical—"A false balance is an abomination to the Lord; but a just weight is His delight." (Proverbs 11:1) Uncertainty analysis is intended to provide information on just how "just" the weight is. Its proper analysis and application are central to a decision process based on experimental results.

Pretest uncertainty analysis tells the experimenter, going in, what to expect. If the uncertainty is too large, it points out those areas that most merit improvement (where the money should be spent).

Example 4-3:

A pretest uncertainty analysis suggests that the uncertainty in the delta pressure measurement across an orifice is ±0.2 psi. The purpose of the experiment is to measure an increase in pressure of 0.15 psi. What is recommended?

What should be done is not run the experiment! An observed change of 0.15 psi might be solely due to the uncertainty. The various error sources should be reviewed to determine the major error contributors (or drivers) and improvements accomplished there before any test of this type is run.

If the bias is too large, the following actions could be taken:

A. Improve the calibration with a better procedure or standards.

B. Utilize independent calibrations. This will help average out bias error in one method.

C. Utilize concomitant variables. If the flow can also be measured with a turbine meter, even an uncertainty of ±0.2 psi on the turbine meter would be adequate for the experimenter to observe a 0.15 psi change. (More on this later in Unit 5.)

D. In-place calibration. The errors that accumulate in a calibration hierarchy can be bypassed sometimes if the calibration standards are brought out to the test site.

If the precision error is too large, the following actions could be taken.

A. Take a larger data set. This will often average out the precision errors, but it is important to take the large data set over the length of variables that contribute most to the precision error. It will do no good, for example, to push the button of the data system, thus acquiring reams of data to average, if the biggest precision errors are day-to-day variations. In that case, many days of data are needed.

B. Get better instrumentation. Instrumentation that is more precise will often help, but this is frequently an expensive solution.

C. Get redundant instrumentation. As discussed earlier, two identical instruments could measure the same parameter or variable and the resultant precision would go down from that of a single instrument by a factor of the square root of two.

D. Apply other techniques (too detailed to discuss here) such as moving averages, data smoothing, regression analysis, etc. Your handy-dandy statistician can help with these.

E. Improve the test design. This is often the easiest. The acquisition of the data, more data, and altering the concentration of data can all help. In the latter case, for example, if the real interest in a test result is the 90% level of a transducer, most of the calibration points should be in that region, not over the whole range of the transducer.

Pretest uncertainty analysis should give the experimenter an idea of where to head. Posttest uncertainty analysis tells the experimenter where he or she has been.

Posttest Uncertainty Estimates

There are several reasons for posttest uncertainty analysis:

A. For future pretest uncertainty analysis. Does the observed precision match the predicted precision? If not, something needs to be learned about the experimental method before it is tried again.

B. Competitive method analysis. Do uncertainties overlap? They should. If they don't, one or both of the uncertainty analyses is wrong and should be investigated.

C. Specifications satisfied? Does the test result with its uncertainty provide data on which decisions can be based?

As an aside, the question should be asked, ''Is the experimental bias error observable in the test result?'' This will be a problem for the student.

Posttest uncertainty analysis tells the experimenter where he or she has been and what to do better the next time. Without it, the experimenter is sailing on a sea of uncertainty with neither a compass (knowledge of bias) nor a rudder (knowledge of precision).

4-9. Conclusion

It should be concluded that uncertainty is a part of all test data, and no test data should be considered without also considering its uncertainty.

References

1. ANSI/ASME PTC 19.1-1985, *Performance Test Code, Instruments and Apparatus, Part I, Measurement Uncertainty*, p. 6.
2. Ibid., p. 11.
3. Ibid., p. 31.

Exercises:

4-1. Terminology Problem

In your own words, define the difference between these three pairs of symbols:

a. ϵ and $2S_X/\sqrt{N}$
b. β and B
c. δ and U

4-2. Pooling Review Problem

Consider the following three standard deviations:

$$s_1 = 40.0, \nu = 12$$
$$s_2 = 50.0, \nu = 15$$
$$s_3 = 30.0, \nu = 7$$

a. What do s_1, s_2 and s_3 represent?
b. What is the best estimate of the population true standard deviation, σ, in the above standard deviations?
c. Calculate the best estimate of the population true standard deviation.
d. What are the degrees of freedom associated with (c) above?

4-3. Delta Problem

Consider the following delta readings between two identical measurement systems.

System 1	System 2
10.3	11.2
9.5	10.5
12.8	13.4

   a. What is the standard deviation for System 1 and for System 2?
   b. Do the results in (a) above represent the correct expected standard deviation for the systems?
   c. Calculate the deltas between the two systems, assuming they are measuring the same process.
   d. Calculate the standard deviation of the deltas.
   e. Obtain the standard deviation for either system (assuming they are identical) from (d) above.
   f. What is learned by comparing (a) and (e) above?

4-4. Interfacility Results Problem

Consider that seven laboratories participate in a round robin experiment. The average result for an orifice calibration is 12.0 lbs/sec for given flow conditions. The standard deviation between laboratories is ±0.2 lbs/sec.
   a. What does the value of 12.0 lbs/sec represent?
   b. What is the laboratory-to-laboratory precision error?
   c. What does (b) above represent from the view of the average for all the laboratories?
   d. What does (b) above represent from the point of view of each laboratory?

4-5. Bias Impact Problem

Consider the elemental bias errors of 1, 2, 3, 10, 20, and 30 psi.
   a. Using Eq. (4-9), obtain the bias limit.
   b. Is (a) above a reasonable estimate of the bias limit? Why or why not?
   c. Using Eq. (4-10), obtain the bias limit.
   d. Is (c) above a reasonable estimate of the bias limit? Why or why not?
   e. Using Eq. (3-7), obtain the bias limit.
   f. Is (f) above a reasonable estimate of the bias limit? Why or why not?

g. *Of (a), (c), and (e) above, which is the best estimate of the bias limit?*

4-6. **Back-to-Back Calibration Problem**

The total uncertainty in a heat transfer measurement is:

Bias limit of the measurement (B) = ±1%
Precision index of the measurement ($S_{\overline{X}}$) = ±1%
Uncertainty = B + $t_{95}S_{\overline{X}}$ = ±3% (large sample sizes)

Half of the bias and precision error is due to calibration, i.e.,

$$B_{CAL} = \pm(1/2)^{1/2}\ \%, \qquad S_{\overline{X}\text{-CAL}} = \pm(1/2)^{1/2}\%$$

a. *For a single test, single calibration, what are the calibration errors, bias and precision?*
b. *For many tests over a period of years involving many calibrations, what are the calibration errors?*
c. *For a back-to-back comparative test where the objective is to determine the difference between two tests with the same instrumentation calibrated once, what are the calibration errors?*
d. *After a period of years, an inspection of the calibration histories shows that this instrumentation drifts with time in a cyclical manner. What would you do about this? Would the above estimates change?*

4-7. **Observable Bias Error Problem**

After a series of tests in an oil refinery, it was determined that the custody transfer of crude from the tanker to the refinery tanks was complete and that the total flow was 1.5 million barrels ±0.5%. The error represents the repeatability of several flow-time integrations that add up to the total.
   a. *What is the uncertainty of the flow measured? (Trick question.)*
   b. *Is the bias component of the uncertainty observable in the test results? Why or why not?*
   c. *What is the risk involved in calling the ±0.5% the flow uncertainty?*

4-8. **Compressor Uncertainty Problem**

As a data validity engineer, you conducted a pretest uncertainty analysis for a compressor rig test. The results were:

Bias limit (B) = 0.4%
Precision index $(S_{\overline{X}})$ = 0.6%
Uncertainty = $B + t_{95}S_{\overline{X}}$ = ±1.6%

The compressor project engineer responsible for the test predicts that the efficiency measured for the new design will be better than the old by 0.9%.

   a. What would you advise?
   b. After the test, plots of data for 10 repeated tests show a scatter band of about ±1.0%. Is this consistent with your analysis?
   c. What can be done to reduce the precision error?
   d. What can be done to reduce the bias error?

Unit 5:
Error Propagation

UNIT 5

Error Propagation

In this unit, you will learn the need and the methods for propagating measurement errors into their effect on the test result. A measurement uncertainty analysis is not complete after the measurement uncertainties of the individual measurements are complete. Their effect on the test result needs to be evaluated. This unit provides the methods for that evaluation.

Learning Objectives — When you have completed this unit, you should:

   A. Understand the need for error propagation.

   B. Understand the theoretical background of error propagation.

   C. Be able to propagate elemental bias and precision errors into a test result.

5-1. General Considerations

It is not enough to evaluate the error magnitudes for the elemental errors or the error magnitudes of the individual measurements such as temperature and pressure. Their combined effect on the test result must be determined. In previous units in this text, the root-sum-square and addition models have been presented as alternatives for the calculation of measurement uncertainty. In every case, the errors being combined were all of the same units, i.e., all temperature, all pressure, or all flow, for example. If a measurement of temperature and pressure yields, through calculation, a flow, combining the temperature and pressure elemental errors cannot be done simply with the methods already presented.

It is in this unit that we propagate the effects of the systematic and random errors for each measurement (i.e., temperature or pressure) into the test result calculated from several measurements.

5-2. The Need for Error Propagation

Combining elemental errors from sources with different units is best accomplished by first converting them to the same units. Usually the simplest and best way to do that is to propagate them into result units. This provides for ease of combination, when the error sources are all expressed in result units, their combination is as simple as shown in the previous units in this text. *This is why error propagation is needed; all the formulae and methods have as their basic assumption of application: identical units only are used.*

For example, suppose there are two precision indexes whose magnitudes and units are $\pm 2.0°F$ and $\pm 3.0°F$. Their combined effect on a test result is computed using Eq. (3-2).

$$S = \pm[\Sigma\Sigma(S_{ij})^2]^{1/2}$$

For one error category, j, this becomes

$$S = \pm[\Sigma(S_i)^2]^{1/2} \qquad (5\text{-}1)$$

Therefore:

$$S = \pm\{[(2.0^2)(°F)^2] + [(3.0^2)(°F)^2]\}^{1/2}$$
$$= \{(13)(°F)^2\}^{1/2}$$
$$= 3.6°F$$

Note that the errors, precision indexes, and the units calculate properly. This is adequate treatment where the combination is linear. Nonlinear equations used to get results must utilize error propagation just as shown below for a linear example with two different units for the precision indexes.

Now consider the case where a result is obtained from the combination of two error sources: one temperature and one pressure. Assuming the temperature precision index is $\pm 2.0°F$ and the pressure precision index is ± 4.5 psia, an attempt is made to use Eq. (5-1) as follows.

$$S = \pm[\Sigma(S_i)^2]^{1/2}$$

In this case, the following is obtained:

$$S = \pm\{[(2.0)^2(°F)^2] + [(3.7)^2(psia)^2]\}^{1/2}$$

As can be seen, the 2.0 and 3.7 might be able to be combined, but what can be done with the °F and psia portions of the above equation? It is necessary to propagate the effects of the two precision indexes into the test result.

Postulating that the result equation has the form of Eq. (5-2), the error propagation may proceed.

$$R = XY \qquad\qquad (5\text{-}2)$$

where X is temperature in degrees F and Y is pressure in psia.

The propagation of error in this result is detailed later under "Taylor's Series for Two Independent Error Sources."

5-3. Theoretical Considerations, the Methods for Error Propagation

There are three well-known methods for error propagation: Taylor's Series (1, 2), "dithering," and Monte Carlo simulation. By far the most commonly utilized is the first; however, it is the aim of all three to convert the units of the error sources (bias and precision) to units of the test result. This is done in each case by determining the *sensitivity* of the test result to error in each source. This sensitivity is sometimes called the *influence coefficient*.

The most common method, Taylor's Series approximation, will be covered in detail. Its derivation, however, and the statistical detail will not be covered here; both References 1 and 2 do that adequately. In addition, numerous statistical texts deal with Taylor's Series approximations.

Taylor's Series Error Propagation

Physical Explanation for the Taylor's Series Error Propagation

In the determination of a quantity that is expressed by a functional relationship of one or more measured variables, a knowledge of the effect of the error in the measurement of the variables on the computed function is often needed. One approach to evaluating the effects of these errors is called Taylor's Series error propagation (3) in which only first-order terms are considered significant.

Briefly, this approach to error propagation proceeds as follows:

Given the function

$$X = F(Y) \qquad (5\text{-}3)$$

it is desired to know the expected error in X due to a known error in Y. One approach is to realize that if the slope of X with reference to Y at some point Y_i could be determined, it would provide an estimate of the effect of small changes in Y about Y_i, (ΔY), would have on X about X_i, (ΔX). This slope is easily evaluated by differentiating X with respect to Y and evaluating the resulting expression at Y_i, i.e.,

$$\text{Slope in X at } Y_i = \frac{\partial F}{\partial Y} \qquad (5\text{-}4)$$

The sign of $(\partial F/\partial Y)$ is an indication of the effect of the sign of the Y error; that is, if $(\partial F/\partial Y)$ is negative, a plus Y error results in a decrease in the value of X.

The effect of this slope is dependent on the error in Y, ΔY at Y_i; in fact, it is seen that:

$$(\Delta X)^2 = (\partial F/\partial Y)^2(\Delta Y)^2 \qquad (5\text{-}5)$$

Here $(\Delta X)^2$ and $(\Delta Y)^2$ are easy to recognize physically as the variance in X and Y, respectively. The above expression is the basis of the Taylor's Series error propagation.

When X is a function of more than one independent variable, that is,

$$X = F(Y,Z) \qquad (5\text{-}6)$$

the statistical procedure is to sum in quadrature:

$$(\Delta X)^2 = (\partial F/\partial Y)^2(\Delta Y)^2 + (\partial F/\partial Z)^2(\Delta Z)^2 \qquad (5\text{-}7)$$

(A similar extension of the equation is used for functions of more than two variables.)

Physically, this could be thought of as the evaluation of the change in two orthogonal variables, Y and Z, with independent error sources, ΔY and ΔZ, and their effect, ΔX, on the dependent variable X through the use of the Pythagorean theorem.

Note that the signs of $(\partial F/\partial Y)$ and $(\partial F/\partial Z)$ are known but then are lost due to squaring and due to incomplete knowledge about the direction of the Y and Z errors. The relative magnitudes of $(\partial F/\partial Y)$ and $(\partial F/\partial Z)$ are an indication of how careful the experimenter must be in the measurement of Y and Z in the regions of Y_i and Z_i.

The proper evaluation of Eq. (5-7) requires only that everything be in the same units. The simplest approach is to evaluate the expression in absolute units and then convert the resulting ΔX into a percent error after summing the individual errors.

Taylor's Series for Two Independent Error Sources

Beginning with an expression for a test result of

$$R = F(X,Y) \qquad\qquad (5\text{-}8)$$

where:

> R = the test result that has a continuous partial derivative and is itself continuous about the point (X,Y)
> X = the first variable that has a continuous error distribution in the region of the point (X,Y)
> Y = the second variable that has a continuous error distribution in the region of the point (X,Y)

The constraints on R, X, and Y are shown in the description of the variables of Eq. (5-8).

The Taylor's Series equation for propagating the effects of errors in X and Y on the result R for independent error sources is:

$$e_R^2 = (\partial R/\partial X)^2(e_X)^2 + (\partial R/\partial Y)^2(e_Y)^2 \qquad (5\text{-}9)$$

where:

> e_R = an error in the result, either bias or precision
> e_X = an error in the measured parameter X, either bias or precision
> e_Y = an error in the measured parameter Y, either bias or precision
> $\delta R/\delta X$ = the influence coefficient that expresses the influence an error in X will have on result R at level X_i

$= \theta_X$, an alternate notation

$\delta R/\delta Y =$ the influence coefficient that expresses the influence an error in Y will have on result R at level Y_i

$= \theta_Y$, an alternate notation

Using Eq. (5-9), the effects of an error in either X or Y may be impressed upon result R. The influence coefficients, evaluated at the X and Y levels of interest, will convert any error, bias, or precision into an error in result R. The influence coefficients are actually the slopes of the error surface at (X_i, Y_i) with respect to either measured parameter, X or Y. The variable e in Eq. (5-9) may be replaced by either bias, B, or the precision index, S. (Remember, $S = s/\sqrt{N}$.) So the effect of the combination of errors from many sources can be computed with an expression such as Eq. (5-9) that is specific for two error sources. The general expression for n error sources is:

$$(e_R)^2 = \sum_{i=1}^{n} [(\partial R/\partial V_i)^2 (e_i)^2] \qquad (5\text{-}10)$$

where:

$V_i =$ the ith measured parameter or variable

$e_i =$ the error (bias or precision) associated with the ith parameter.

In addition, the use of the sensitivity coefficients permits the root sum squaring of the error components since, once multiplied by their individual influence coefficients, each is in the units of results. In other words, the square root of Eq. (5-10) is the error in R due to errors in the measured parameters that go to make up R. (In case you are interested, the units of each influence coefficient are [(results)/(variable of interest)].) This capability of the influence coefficients is central to error propagation, which could not be accomplished without it.

Remember that one assumption of this approach is that the error sources in X and Y are independent.

Step-By-Step Approach to Simple Error Propagation, Two Measured Parameters, Independent Error Sources

To get an idea of how this approach works, consider the result Eq. (5-2):

$$R = XY$$

In this expression, the result, R, is dependent on the measurement of X (in, for example, degrees) and Y (in, for example, psi).

The error propagation steps to follow are:

A. Write the closed form expression for the result as has been done in Eq. (5-2).

B. Derive the influence coefficients (or sensitivity) with partial differentiation.

C. Evaluate the magnitudes of the influence coefficients at the point of interest, (X_i, Y_i).

D. Fill in Eq. (5-9) with the appropriate values and calculate the error in R caused by the errors in X and Y.

E. Compute the percent error in R last, at the R level of interest.

Now for the example of Eq. (5-2), the sensitivities are as follows:

$$\theta_X = \partial R / \partial X = Y \qquad (5\text{-}11)$$
$$\theta_Y = \partial R / \partial Y = X \qquad (5\text{-}12)$$

Assuming the bias error for X is 2.0°F and the bias error for Y is 3.7 psia, the following is obtained using Eq. (5-10) in the region of (150 degrees, 45 psia):

$$
\begin{aligned}
B_R &= [(Y^2)(B_X)^2 + (X^2)(B_Y)^2]^{1/2} \\
&= [(45^2)(2)^2 + (150^2)(3.7^2)]^{1/2} \\
&= [8100 + 308{,}025]^{1/2} \\
&= 562°\text{F-psia} \qquad (5\text{-}13)
\end{aligned}
$$

Since the R level of interest here is $(150°F)(45\ psia) = 6750°F$-psia, the percent error in R is $(562/6750)(100) = 8.3\%$.

Note that the percent bias errors in X and Y were 1.3% and 8.2%. Were these to be simply root-sum-squared, the result error in R would have been 9.0%, definitely the wrong answer. Proper error propagation in absolute units is an important step in uncertainty analysis. It is not possible to merely combine percent errors.

Note also that Eq. (5-13) maybe used to identify the error source of significance. It reveals the major contributor to error in the result as Y, not X. It would not pay the experimenter to work hard and spend money improving the temperature measurement. Almost all the error is caused by the pressure measurement error. This is where the improvements should be concentrated if the predicted error in the result of 8.3% is unacceptable.

(Here is the usual place where Prato charts are used to make clear the major error sources. Most statistics texts discuss Prato charts.)

Taylor's Series for Two Nonindependent Error Sources

It is sometimes the case that the error sources are not independent. That is, one is correlated to some extent with another. In this case, it is not possible to use the error propagation equations just shown. Consider the example of Eq. (5-2):

$$R = XY$$

The general expression for error propagation, Eq. (5-10), does not apply. That expression was for independent error sources in X and Y. However, we are saved by the mathematician again; the more general formula for error propagation with a Taylor's Series for two variables is:

$$(e_R)^2 = \sum_{i=1}^{n} \{[(\partial R/\partial V_i)^2(e_i)^2] + [\text{all cross product terms}]\}$$

$$(5\text{-}14)$$

where V_i = the ith measured parameter or variable. Cross-product terms have two variables in each and are generically shown as:

$$[2(\partial R/\partial V_a)(\partial R/\partial V_b)\rho_{ab}e_a e_b]$$

where:

> a and b = the complete set of combinations of two
>   variables
> e_a and e_b = the error in variables a and b
> ρ_{ab} = the correlation of error in a on error in b

$$\text{Note that } \rho_{ab} = \frac{\{n[\Sigma(a_i b_i)] - (\Sigma a_i)(\Sigma b_i)\}}{\{[n(\Sigma a_i^2) - (\Sigma a_i)^2][n(\Sigma b_i^2) - (\Sigma b_i)^2]\}^{1/2}} \quad (5\text{-}15)$$

Here, too, the variables a and b represent all combinations of two variables from the general expression for the error propagation formula, Eq. (5-14). A complete set of these terms for two variables is shown in Eq. (5-16) and for three variables in Eq. (5-19).

Step-By-Step Approach to Simple Error Propagation, Two Measured Parameters, Nonindependent Error Sources

To get an idea of how this approach works, consider the result Eq. (5-2):

$$R = XY$$

In this expression, the result, R, is dependent on the measurement of X (in, for example, degrees) and Y (in, for example, psi).

The error propagation steps are as follows:

A. Write the closed form expression for the result as has been done in Eq. (5-2).

B. Derive the influence coefficients (or sensitivities) with partial differentiation.

C. Evaluate the magnitudes of the influence coefficients at the point of interest, (X_i, Y_i).

D. Fill in Eq. (5-14) with the appropriate values and calculate the error in R caused by the errors in X and Y.

E. Compute the percent error in R last, at the R level of interest.

Now for the example of Eq. (5-2), the sensitivities remain as before and are, as in Eqs. (5-11) and (5-12):

$$\theta_X = \partial R / \partial X = Y$$
$$\theta_Y = \partial R / \partial Y = X$$

Applying Eq. (5-14) and assuming the correlation between X and Y is 1.0, the following is obtained:

$$e_R^2 = (\partial R / \partial X)^2 (e_X)^2 + (\partial R / \partial Y)^2 (e_Y)^2 + 2(\partial R / \partial X)(\partial R / \partial Y)\rho_{XY} e_X e_Y$$

$$(5\text{-}16)$$

where:

e_R = an error in the result either bias or precision

e_X = an error in the measured parameter X, either bias or precision

e_Y = an error in the measured parameter Y, either bias or precision

ρ_{XY} = the correlation of the error in X on the error in Y

From Eq. (5-16) and remembering that the bias errors are $\pm 2.0°F$ for X and ± 3.7 psia for Y, using the correlation term of 1.0 and the levels of interest for X and Y as 45°F and 150 psia, respectively, the following is obtained:

$$\begin{aligned} B_R &= [(Y^2)(B_X)^2 + (X^2)(B_Y)^2 + 2YX\rho_{XY}B_XB_Y]^{1/2} \\ &= [(45^2)(2)^2 + (150^2)(3.7^2) \\ &\quad + 2(150)(45)(1.0)(2.0)(3.7)]^{1/2} \\ &= [8100 + 308{,}025 + 99900]^{1/2} \\ &= 645°F\text{-psia} \end{aligned}$$

$$(5\text{-}17)$$

Since the R level of interest here is $(150°F)(45 \text{ psia}) = 6750°F\text{-}$psia, the percent error in R is $(645/6750)(100) = 9.6\%$. This is a significantly larger error than would have been obtained if the error dependency had been ignored.

Additional Example of Step-By-Step Instructions

Consider now the result Eq. (5-2):

$$R = X / Y$$

From Eqs. (5-11) and (5-12), the sensitivities are:

$$\theta_X = \partial R/\partial X = 1/Y \qquad = 0.022222$$
$$\theta_Y = \partial R/\partial Y = -X/Y^2 \quad = -0.074074$$

Applying Eq. (5-16) and again remembering that the bias errors are $\pm 2.0°F$ for X and ± 3.7 psia for Y, using the correlation term of 1.0 and the levels of interest for X and Y as 45°F and 150 psia, respectively, the following is obtained:

$$
\begin{aligned}
B_R &= [(1/Y)^2(B_X)^2 + (-X/Y^2)^2(B_Y)^2 \\
&\quad + 2(1/Y)(-X/Y^2)\rho_{XY}B_XB_Y]^{1/2} \\
&= [(0.022222^2)(2^2) + (-0.074074^2)(3.7^2) \\
&\quad + 2(0.022222)(-0.074074)(1.0)(2.0)(3.7)]^{1/2} \\
&= [0.0019753 + 0.0751164 - 0.0243619]^{1/2} \\
&= 0.23°F/psia
\end{aligned}
$$

Since the R level of interest here is $(150°F)/(45 \text{ psia}) = 3.33°F/\text{psia}$, the percent error in R is $(0.23)(100)/3.33 = 6.97\%$. This is obviously a significantly smaller error than would have been obtained if the error dependency had been ignored. Ignoring the dependency or correlation would have resulted in using only the first two terms of the equation, that is, $(0.0019753 + 0.0751164)^{1/2}(100)/(3.33) = 8.34\%$. Indeed, some of the error in the result disappears when there is perfect correlation between the two error sources for the given result equation.

It should be noted that the above methods for nonindependent error sources may be applied to error sources that are partially dependent ($|\rho| > 0.0$) although not completely nonindependent ($|\rho| = 1.0$). Note that ρ, the correlation coefficient, may vary from -1.0 to $+1.0$. A negative correlation coefficient implies that the second variable is inversely correlated with the first. This means that an increase in the second variable, or error source, will produce a decrease in the first. A positive correlation coefficient means that the second variable is directly correlated to the first. In this case, an increase in the second variable will result in an increase in the first variable as well.

Application to Three Variables

It is instructive to see the equations that apply to a three-variable system. In this way, all the permutations associated with Eq. (5-14), specifically the cross-product terms, are written out. For a three-variable system then, with nonindependent error sources, the error propagation equation is as follows in Eq. (5-18). The result equation is Eq. (5-19).

$$R = f(X,Y,Z) \tag{5-18}$$

$$
\begin{aligned}
e_R^2 = {}& (\partial R/\partial X)^2 (e_X)^2 + (\partial R/\partial Y)^2 (e_Y)^2 + (\partial R/\partial Z)^2 (e_Z)^2 \\
& + 2(\partial R/\partial X)(\partial R/\partial Y)\rho_{XY}e_X e_Y \\
& + 2(\partial R/\partial X)(\partial R/\partial Z)\rho_{XZ}e_X e_Z \\
& + 2(\partial R/\partial Z)(\partial R/\partial Y)\rho_{ZY}e_Z e_Y
\end{aligned} \tag{5-19}
$$

where:

e_R = an error in the result, either bias or precision
e_X = an error in the measured parameter X, either bias or precision
e_Y = an error in the measured parameter Y, either bias or precision
e_Z = an error in the measured parameter Z, either bias or precision
ρ_{XY} = the correlation of the error in X on the error in Y
ρ_{XZ} = the correlation of the error in X on the error in Z
ρ_{ZY} = the correlation of the error in Z on the error in Y

One can see how complex this can get. However, simply being careful to follow the rules of mathematics will result in a proper error propagation. Note that, when the error sources are independent, all the correlation coefficients, ρ, are zero, so only the first three terms of Eq. (5-18) remain for the independent case.

"Dithering" for Error Propagation

In the era of modern super computers, problems can be solved that have no closed-form equation as their solution. The closed-form equation permits the Taylor's Series approach to error propagation. Without that closed form, there is no way to perform a Taylor's Series error propagation.

Word of Advice about Dithering and the Need To Do It

The author's advice on this is, "Who needs it!" In every case encountered by this author where there were extensive, detailed, highly intelligent, complex, and lengthy expressions that required some iteration to solve, there was also in "your standard college text" a closed-form equation that would yield the correct result within a few percent of the expensive, long, and tiresome super computer method. While the long and tiresome computer methods are required for obtaining the most precise solutions (say, an error in the equation of 2 or 3 percent was intolerable), the college text expression would yield the result to a few percent and an uncertainty analysis to likewise a few percent. That is, no one cares if the error in the error analysis is 10 percent. Many people do care if the value calculated for the result is in error by 10 percent. Therefore, continue your extensive computer simulations and overnight giga-mega bit runs for your test result, but try the college text simple expression for the basis of the error propagation. You'll likely find it works just fine.

"Dithering" Method

"Dithering" error propagation is a long process that proceeds approximately as follows. The computer software used to calculate the test or experimental result is used to calculate the result. Then, in turn, a convenient amount of each variable's error (bias and/or precision) is added to the input data to the software, and a new test result is calculated. The difference (between the new result and the old result) divided by the error increment used is the sensitivity of the result to error in that parameter at that result level. (The convenient amount of error added is usually 1%, 0.1%, 10°F, 1.0 psia, etc. It should approximate the expected bias and/or precision, and its effect should be evaluated at or near each variable's level of interest as the slopes of equations can sometimes change significantly with a variable change of only a few percent.)

This process is repeated for all the error sources, and the resulting sensitivities are tabulated. The final uncertainty analysis is then computed by root-sum-squaring the bias (and later the precision) errors times their sensitivities to obtain the result uncertainty, Eq. (5-14).

Monte Carlo Simulation

This method of error propagation is even more difficult than "dithering." Again, the computer software needed to obtain a test result is used. However, in this case, error distributions are posed for all error sources, bias and precision. A random number generator then selects a value from those distributions for each type of error source, and the resulting errors are totaled. This process is repeated hundreds or thousands of times until a distribution of error in the test result is developed. The limits of this distribution are the uncertainty analysis.

This process is not recommended. It is complicated, difficult, and almost always not needed.

5-4. Error Propagation Examples

Simple Propagation Example, Independent Error Sources, Series Flowmeter Network

Given that the flow in a facility is measured by three turbine flowmeters in series, each one of which has the same uncertainty. The best estimate of the facility flow is the average flow reported by the three meters. This condition is illustrated as follows.

Total flow $\rightarrow$ |meter A| $\rightarrow$ |meter B| $\rightarrow$ |meter C| $\rightarrow$ Total flow

That is:

$$F = (A + B + C)/3$$
$$= A/3 + B/3 + C/3 \tag{5-20}$$

where:

F = the average facility flow
A = the flow according to meter A
B = the flow according to meter B
C = the flow according to meter C

Utilizing Eq. (5-10) for either precision or bias error, the following is obtained, assuming independent errors:

$$(e_F)^2 = [(\partial F/\partial A)^2 (e_A)^2] + [(\partial F/\partial B)^2 (e_B)^2]$$
$$+ [(\partial F/\partial C)^2 (e_C)^2] \qquad (5\text{-}21)$$

where e_X = the error in F, A, B, or C (precision or bias).

Substituting the partial derivatives, the following error equation is obtained:

$$(e_F)^2 = (e_A/3)^2 + (e_B/3)^2 + (e_C/3)^2$$
$$= (1/9)(e_A^2 + e_B^2 + e_C^2)$$

This is the simple case of linear addition models.

The case for parallel flowmeter networks is left as an exercise for the student; that is, what is the error propagation equation for three meters in parallel measuring the total flow? (Exercise 5-5.)

Detailed Error Propagation Example, Some Errors Correlated, Compressor Efficiency

Consider the example of the calculation of the measurement uncertainty of the efficiency measurement of a compressor. This task may be divided into several steps:

A. The defining equation for compressor efficiency

B. Making an error source summary

C. Defining the elemental pressure and temperature errors

D. Propagating the errors with Taylor's Series

E. Compiling an uncertainty analysis summary

These steps will now be handled in turn.

Step 1. The defining equation for compressor efficiency. The textbook definition of compressor efficiency is entirely adequate for this analysis. True, compressor designers have very detailed and fancy computer routines for this calculation, but that is not needed for a credible uncertainty analysis. The textbook expression will contain all the main actors that contribute error to the compressor efficiency calculation. That equation is:

$$\eta_c = [(P_2/P_1)^{(1-1/\gamma)} - 1]/[(T_2/T_1) - 1] \qquad (5\text{-}22)$$

where:

η_c = compressor efficiency
P_1 = inlet pressure, nominally 14.7 psia
P_2 = exit pressure, nominally 96.0 psia
T_1 = inlet temperature, nominally 520°R
T_2 = exit temperature, nominally 970°R
γ = ratio of specific heats, nominally 1.40

(Note that the example levels for data in this example are the same as those in Reference 4.)

Step 2. Making an error source summary. The next step in the uncertainty analysis is summarizing the error sources and their magnitudes. For simplicity, this example will detail the temperature measurement errors and only outline the pressure measurement errors.

The pressure and temperature measurement errors may be summarized as shown in Table 5-1. These are the error estimates that apply to each measurement of each of the above parameters.

Note that in this error uncertainty analysis the simplifying assumption has been made that all the precision errors are S and are obtained from enough data. Table 5-1 is only a summary of previous work. To fully understand the uncertainty analysis process, it is necessary to consider the elemental errors and their magnitudes. This will be done for temperature only in this example, and are shown in Table 5-2.

Parameter	Bias	Precision Index	Degrees of Freedom
T_1	± 0.80°R	± 0.60°R	32
T_2	± 1.60°R	± 0.70°R	38
P_1	± 0.02 psia	± 0.03 psia	45
P_2	± 0.17 psia	± 0.17 psia	24

Table 5-1. Summarized Pressure and Temperature Measurement Error Sources and Magnitudes

Error Source	Bias	Precision Index ($S_{\bar{x}}$)	Degrees of Freedom $(n - 1)$	N+
Inlet temperature (T_1):				
TC* wire variability	±0.50°R	±0.20°R	45	1
Secondary TC reference	±0.50°R	±0.20°R	8	1
Ice reference	±0.07°R	±0.02°R	3	1
Data acquisition system	±0.40°R	±0.50°R	20	5
Root sum square	±0.82°R(cr)	±0.57°R	32**	
Exit temperature (T_2):				
All inlet errors	±0.82°R(cr)	±0.57°R	32	1
TC probe variability	±1.00°R	±0.30°R	16	1
Thermocouple drift	±1.00°R	±0.20°R	1	1
Root sum square	±1.63°R	±0.67°R	38++	

*TC = Thermocouple

**Actually 32.5, but truncating is proper for Welch-Satterthwaite degrees of freedom. Its calculation is left as an exercise for the reader.

+N, this is the number of readings averaged at this hierarchy level. It is already in $S_{\bar{x}}$.

++Actually 38.3, but truncating is proper for Welch-Satterthwaite degrees of freedom. Its calculation is left as an exercise for the student.

(cr) These two errors are identical; they are perfectly correlated ($\rho = +1.00$). This portion of the errors must be treated specially in a Taylor's Series approach.

Table 5-2. Temperature Elemental Measurement Errors

Note with care that the precision error quoted is the precision error of the mean, $S_{\bar{x}}$, not just the precision of the data, S_X. It is the precision index of the mean that is used in error propagation and in the Welch-Satterthwaite formula for combining degrees of freedom.

Step 3. Defining the elemental errors. Tables 5-1 and 5-2 have both precision and bias errors already defined. Note that the degrees of freedom are also noted for each of the precision indexes. This is a vital part of the uncertainty analysis, for without those degrees of freedom, the proper t-statistic cannot be determined, and no uncertainty statement can be framed.

It is important to note that the exit temperature errors have a portion of their bias errors that are dependent or correlated. These are the errors that are identical to the errors in the inlet temperature measurements. Note that the same inlet temperature precision errors also show up in the exit temperature error summary but are not correlated with those of the inlet temperature. Why?

Precision errors, although from the same error source, are never correlated or related. The fact that they have the same factor as their origin and the same magnitude does not make them correlated or dependent or related. The reason is that precision errors cause a change in the test data every time they have a chance to do so. In addition, once done, the next opportunity has no relationship with the previous opportunity; precision errors are random. Precision indexes set bounds only on their distribution.

Bias error, however, if it shows up more than once in an experiment, will do so at the same magnitude and sign each time. Here, the error source is the same and the error impact is identical. After all, the definition for bias, or systematic, error is that it does not change for the duration of the experiment or test.

It is for this reason that the $\pm 0.82\,°F$ bias error in Table 5-2 is listed for both the root sum square of the inlet errors and the "All inlet errors" term of the exit temperature error summary. It is the same, perfectly correlated as it is identical, error. The correlation coefficient is $+1.00$.

In an error analysis, therefore, it is important to separate those errors that are not dependent and those that are dependent, or correlated, or related. (Note here that correlation does not imply relationship, only correlation. This will be discussed later in Section 7-5.)

Throughout Tables 5-1 and 5-2, the error in γ, the ratio of specific heats, is considered negligible. This is the kind of assumption that makes the use of Taylor's Series for error propagation easy and yet sufficient for determining the measurement uncertainty with adequate correctness.

Step 4. Propagating Errors with Taylor's Series. The next step in the uncertainty analysis is to propagate the pressure and temperature errors into results units of efficiency.

To propagate the effects of the temperature and pressure errors into efficiency units requires determining the partial derivatives of the efficiency equation with respect to four variables or parameters: inlet temperature, inlet pressure, exit temperature, and exit pressure.

Using Eq. (5-14), the following sensitivities, or θ's, are obtained.

$$\theta_{T_1} = \frac{(T_2)\{[(P_2/P_1)^{[(\gamma-1)/\gamma]}] - 1\}}{[(T_2 - T_1)^2]} = +0.00340 \qquad (5\text{-}23)$$

$$\theta_{T_2} = \frac{(-T_1)\{[(P_2/P_1)^{[(\gamma-1)/\gamma]}] - 1\}}{[(T_2 - T_1)^2]} = -0.00182 \qquad (5\text{-}24)$$

$$\theta_{P_1} = \frac{-[(\gamma-1)/\gamma][(P_2/P_1)^{-1/\gamma}][P_2/(P_1)^2]}{[(T_2/T_1) - 1]} = -0.03839 \quad (5\text{-}25)$$

$$\theta_{P_2} = \frac{[(\gamma-1)/\gamma](1/P_1)[(P_2/P_1)^{-1/\gamma}]}{[(T_2/T_1) - 1]} = +0.00588 \qquad (5\text{-}26)$$

It is now convenient to summarize the error sources, their magnitudes, their parameters' nominal levels, and their sensitivities or influence coefficients. This is done in Table 5-3.

It is important to note that the bias limits and the precision indexes are in the same units as the error sources, or parameters, *and that they are for one measurement of each parameter.* The sensitivities are in the units of [efficiency/(error source units)]. In this way, the sensitivities times the errors will yield the effect of that error source in efficiency units. Those results may then be combined in root-sum-square methodology to yield the bias limit and the precision index for the test or experiment.

Utilizing Eq. (5-24), the following expressions for bias limit and precision index are obtained.

Error Source	Level (Units)	Bias Limit	Precision Indexes	Degrees of Freedom	Sensitivity
T_1	520 (°R)	0.80	0.60	32	+0.00340
T_2	970 (°R)	1.60	0.70	38	−0.00182
P_1	14.7 (psia)	0.02	0.03	45	−0.03839
P_2	96.0 (psia)	0.17	0.17	24	+0.00588

Table 5-3. Error and Source Summary

The bias limit for efficiency in efficiency units is:

$$B_\eta = [(\Theta_{T_1})^2(B_{T_1})^2 + (\Theta_{T_2})^2(B_{T_2})^2 + (\Theta_{P_1})^2(B_{P_1})^2$$

$$+ (\Theta_{P_2})^2(B_{P_2})^2 + 2\Theta_{T_1}\Theta_{T_2}\rho(B_{T_1})^*(B_{T_2})^*]^{1/2} \qquad (5\text{-}27)$$

$$= [(0.00340)^2(0.80)^2 + (-0.00182)^2(1.60)^2$$

$$+ (-0.03839)^2(0.02)^2 + (0.00588)^2(0.17)^2$$

$$+ (2)(0.00340)(-0.00182)(1.00)(0.80)(0.80)]^{1/2}$$

$$= (7.3984 \times 10^{-6} + 8.47974 \times 10^{-6}$$

$$+ 0.58951 \times 10^{-6} + 0.99920 \times 10^{-6} - 7.92064 \times 10^{-6})^{1/2}$$

$$B_\eta = (9.56442 \times 10^{-6})^{1/2} = 0.0031 \text{ efficiency units}$$

Note that the asterisk (*) indicated the use of only the correlated portion of the bias limit. [Occasionally the notation $\hat{B}$ is used instead of the asterisk (*).] That is, for this experiment, the 0.80°R is the same or identical for both the inlet and exit temperatures. For those bias limits, the correlation coefficient, ρ, is +1.00.

The expression for the precision index for the test or experiment has exactly the same form:

$$S_\eta = [(\Theta_{T_1})^2(S_{T_1})^2 + (\Theta_{T_2})^2(S_{T_2})^2 + (\Theta_{P_1})^2(S_{P_1})^2$$

$$+ (\Theta_{P_2})^2(S_{P_2})^2] \qquad (5\text{-}28)$$

$$= [(0.00340)^2(0.60)^2 + (-0.00182)^2(0.70)^2$$

$$+ (-0.03839)^2(0.03)^2 + (0.00588)^2(0.17)^2]$$

$$= (4.16160 \times 10^{-6} + 1.62308 \times 10^{-6}$$

$$+ 1.32641 \times 10^{-6} + 0.99920 \times 10^{-6})^{1/2}$$

$$S_\eta = (7.11109 \times 10^{-6})^{1/2} = 0.0027 \text{ efficiency units}$$

Note that the correlation term (or cross-product term) is zero in Eq. (5-21). This is because the correlation coefficient for the precision errors of the same source is always zero. They always have an independent effect on the uncertainty analysis. Once having occurred, the next opportunity does not know how the last one came out. This is unlike the bias terms of Eq. (5-27).

The uncertainty still cannot be computed because the degrees of freedom associated with S_η has not been determined. This is necessary in order to select the Student's t from the table in Appendix D. The degrees of freedom is determined with the Welch-Satterthwaite formula, Eq. (3-6).

$$\nu = \frac{[\Sigma(\theta_j S_j)^2]^2}{\{\Sigma[(\theta_j S_j)^4 / \nu_j]\}}$$

Using the precision indexes and sensitivities in Table 5-3, the following is obtained:

$$\nu = (50.5676 \times 10^{-12})/(0.691239 \times 10^{-12})$$
$$= 73.2 \approx 73 \text{ (always truncate)}$$

For 73 degrees of freedom, t = 2.00. The measurement uncertainty is then computed as follows:

$$U_{ADD} = \pm[0.0031 + (2.00 \times 0.0027)] = \pm0.0085 \text{ efficiency units}$$
$$(3\text{-}10)$$

$$U_{RSS} = \pm[(0.0031)^2 + (2.00 \times 0.0027)^2]^{1/2}$$
$$= \pm0.0062 \text{ efficiency units} \qquad (3\text{-}14)$$

The calculation of uncertainty for the efficiency measurement is now complete. If it is desired to know the percent uncertainty, now is the time to calculate that. The efficiency level is 0.8198 $\pm$ 0.0085, or 0.8198 $\pm$ 1.04% for U_{ADD}.

When multiple measurements of a parameter are made (M times), the above tSj values would need to be divided by $\sqrt{M}$ before they are root-sum-squared. This accounts for the averaging of several measurements of the parameter.

If the experiment is repeated $\mathfrak{M}$ times, the S_n would be divided by $\sqrt{\mathfrak{M}}$ before it is used in the random error component of the uncertainty.

Example 5-1:
Suppose there were 20 T_1, 10 T_2, 15 P_1, and 5 P_2 measurements for each result and that the whole experiment were repeated 3 times. The uncertainty would then be calculated as follows:

$$B_\eta = 0.0031 \text{ efficiency units (as before)}$$

$$S_\eta = (4.16160 \times 10^{-6}/\sqrt{20} + 1.62308 \times 10^{-6}/\sqrt{10}$$
$$+ 1.3264 \times 10^{-6}/\sqrt{15} + 0.99920 \times 10^{-6}/\sqrt{5})^{1/2}$$
$$= [(0.93056 + 0.51326 + 0.34248 + 0.44686) \times 10^{-6}]^{1/2}$$
$$= 0.0015 \text{ efficiency units}$$

$$U_{ADD} = \pm[0.0031 + (2.00 \times 0.0015/\sqrt{3})]$$
$$= \pm0.0048 \text{ efficiency units} \tag{5-29}$$

$$U_{RSS} = \pm[(0.0031)^2 + (2.00 \times 0.0015/\sqrt{3})^2]^{1/2}$$
$$= \pm0.0037 \text{ efficiency units} \tag{5-30}$$

The result uncertainty using either Eqs. (5-29) or (5-30) is significantly lower than that obtained without the repeat testing and shown in Eqs. (3-10) or (3-14). Note that replicate measurements do not reduce the impact of bias at all.

5-5. Summary

Error propagation, then, is required to evaluate the effect of error sources on a test result where either the error sources have different units or the result is in units that are different from the error sources. The easiest method for error propagation is to use the "college text" closed-form solution for the experimental test result and a Taylor's Series error propagation approach.

References

1. ANSI/ASME PTC 19.1-1985, *Instruments and Apparatus, Part I, Measurement Uncertainty*, pages 57–60.
2. Coleman, H. W., and Steele, Jr., W. G., *Experimentation and Uncertainty Analysis for Engineers*, pages 189–199 (John Wiley & Sons, 1989).
3. Ku, Harry H., NBS Report No. 9011, *Notes on the Use of Propagation of Error Formulas*, 1965.
4. Ob cit., pages 41–44.

Exercises:

5-1. *What is the purpose of error propagation?*

5-2. *Orifice Problem*

		Given Test Pressure Data for an Orifice			
Point#	(P_{up})	(P_{dn})	Point#	(P_{up})	(P_{dn})
1	6.80	5.30	6	9.70	8.20
2	11.70	10.50	7	7.40	6.10
3	4.10	2.75	8	3.85	2.05
4	10.35	9.00	9	7.95	6.20
5	11.95	10.55	10	10.10	8.85

    a. Compute the standard deviation of the upstream pressures, $S_{P_{up}}$, and the downstream pressures, $S_{P_{dn}}$.

    b. Using $\Delta P = P_{up} - P_{dn}$,

        1) Obtain Taylor's series for $S_{\Delta P_{ind}}$ (assume P_{up} and P_{dn} are independent).

        2) Calculate $S_{\Delta P}$ with equations from 1) above (start with $S_{P_{up}}$ and $S_{P_{dn}}$).

        3) Obtain Taylor's series for $S_{\Delta P_{dep}}$ (assume P_{up} and P_{dn} are dependent).

        4) Calculate $S_{\Delta P}$ with equations from 3) above (again use $S_{P_{up}}$ and $S_{P_{dn}}$). Note, r = 0.9983.

        5) Calculate the 10 ΔP values.

        6) Calculate $S_{\Delta P}$ from the ΔP values.

        7) Compare 6) with 4) and 2). What is learned?

5-3. Word Problem

Aircraft in-flight net thrust equals engine gross thrust minus inlet drag. Measured airflow is a factor in calculating both drag and gross thrust. What problems does this produce in estimating the errors in net thrust?

5-4. Calculate the degrees of freedom associated with the two root-sum-square precision index results in Table 5-2 shown as 32 and 38.

5-5. What is the error propagation equation for three meters in parallel measuring the total flow? That is:

$$\text{total flow} \rightarrow \begin{vmatrix} \rightarrow |\text{meter A}| \rightarrow \\ \rightarrow |\text{meter B}| \rightarrow \\ \rightarrow |\text{meter C}| \rightarrow \end{vmatrix} \rightarrow \text{total flow}$$

5-6. Decision Time

    a. What is more accurate (lower uncertainty)—total flow measured with three meters in series or with three meters in parallel? Assume all precision errors are ± 1 gal/min and that all bias errors are independent and are ± 1 gal/min.

b. Which method is more accurate if all the bias errors are the same exact error source, that is, perfectly correlated?

Unit 6:
Weighting Method for
Multiple Results

UNIT 6

Weighting Method for Multiple Results

This unit addresses weighting several independent measurements in order to obtain a final test result that is more accurate than any of the individual measurements. It is a technique that is valuable where no one measurement method is adequate for the measurement uncertainty desired.

Learning Objectives — When you have completed this unit, you should:

A. Understand the purpose of multiple test results.

B. Know the principles for calculating a final result that is weighted by the uncertainty of the several test results.

C. Be able to compute a final result by weighting, which is more accurate than any of the individual results used.

6-1. The Purpose of Multiple Measurements of the Same Test Result

It has been said that "*the purpose for making redundant measurements is so the experimenter can choose the result he wants*" (1). Redundant, independent measurements of the same test result, when used properly, can yield a test result that is more accurate than any of the redundant measurements. This may be difficult to believe, but it is true. It is actually possible to average two measurements of the same results and get a final average result more accurate than either of the two. For example, if one measurement uncertainty is ±1.0% and the second is ±2.0%, the weighted result will have a lower uncertainty than ±1.0%. This unit describes the weighting procedure, which will yield results with improved uncertainty when there is more than one measurement of the same result.

6-2. Fundamentals of Weighting by Uncertainty

A necessary condition for weighting results by their uncertainty is that the competing measurements be nondependent. A standard methodology for weighting competing results is found in many statistics texts (2) and is covered in the national uncertainty standard (3). The basic principles and approach will be covered in this unit.

Assumptions for this method are as follows:

A. More than one measurement of the same result is made by different methods.

B. The competing measurements are nondependent.

C. Each measurement method has its own, nondependent, uncertainty.

Fundamental Equations

There is a direct comparison between obtaining test results with weighted and without weighted averages. There are standard formulas for average, weighted average, bias, weighted bias, precision, weighted precision, degrees of freedom, and weighted degrees of freedom. These formulas will be presented with direct comparison to the usual formulas, which are unweighted.

Averages

The standard formula for an average of several measurements is:

$$\text{Average} = \overline{X} = \frac{\sum\limits_{i=1}^{N} X_i}{N} \tag{6-1}$$

However, a better average may be obtained from several independent (nondependent) measurements of the same test result, using a weighted average.

The formula for the weighted average, $\underline{\underline{X}}$, is:

$$\text{Weighted Average} = \underline{\underline{X}} = \sum\limits_{i=1}^{n} W_i \overline{X}_i \tag{6-2}$$

where:

$$W_i = \frac{(1/u_i)^2}{\displaystyle\sum_{i=1}^{n}[(1/u_i)^2]} \tag{6-3}$$

u_i = the uncertainty of the ith measurement method.

In this approach, the weighting is inversely proportional to the uncertainty of the method. That this is correct is intuitive. The most accurate single method, lowest uncertainty, should count the most. This approach does that.

For the case of two nondependent measurement methods yielding two nondependent test results, the situation is schematically as shown in Fig. 6-1. Here, two different result averages can be obtained—one by the standard averaging technique, Eq. (6-1), and the other by weighting, Eq. (6-2). *When weighting is used, the resulting average will be known to greater accuracy (lower uncertainty) than even the best (lowest uncertainty) method employed.*

For the simple case of only two measurement methods, the weights are:

$$W_1 = (1/u_1)^2/[(1/u_1)^2 + (1/u_2)^2] \tag{6-4}$$

$$= (u_2)^2/[(u_1)^2 + (u_2)^2]$$

$$W_2 = (u_1)^2/[(u_1)^2 + (u_2)^2] \tag{6-5}$$

Note that the sum of the weights W_1 and W_2 is unity.

$$W_1 + W_2 = 1.00 \tag{6-6}$$

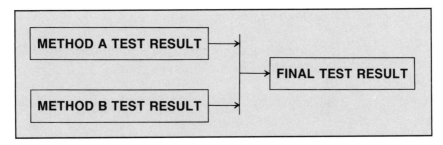

Fig. 6-1. The Case of Two Nondependent Measurement Methods of a Single Test Result

This is true for all weights for an experiment, no matter how many there are. It is a good check on the correct computation of weights or weighting factors.

Once the weighting factors are calculated, it is then possible to compute the uncertainty. Both weighted bias and weighted precision must be obtained and combined to obtain the weighted result's uncertainty.

Weighted Bias Terms

Reference 3 contains the equations used to obtain the weighted bias.

The usual calculation of bias is done with Eq. (3-7):

$$B = \pm[\Sigma\Sigma(b_{ij})^2]^{1/2}$$

Eq. (3-7) is used when all bias elemental errors, b_{ij}, are the same units; they are in the units of the results. The influence coefficients are unity and are implicit in the equation. The more general form of Eq. (3-7) is Eq. (6-7), where the influence coefficients, or sensitivity coefficients, Θ_{ij}, are shown explicitly.

$$B = \pm[\Sigma\Sigma(\Theta_{ij})^2(b_{ij})^2]^{1/2} \qquad (6\text{-}7)$$

Extending Eq. (6-7) to the case of weighted bias, the following formula is obtained:

$$\underline{\underline{B}} = \pm[\Sigma\Sigma(W_{ij})^2(\Theta_{ij})^2(b_{ij})^2]^{1/2} \qquad (6\text{-}8)$$

Eq. (6-8) is the expression that is used to compute the weighted bias error to be associated with the weighted test result. The weighted bias is $\underline{\underline{B}}$.

Weighted Precision Terms

Reference 3 also contains the equations used to obtain the weighted precision.

The usual calculation of the precision index is done with Eq. (3-3):

$$S = \pm[\Sigma\Sigma(S_{ij})^2]^{1/2}$$

Eq. (3-3) is used when all precision indexes, S_{ij}, are the same units; they are in the units of the results. The influence coefficients are unity and are implicit in the equation. The more general form of Eq. (3-3) is Eq. (6-9), where the influence coefficients, or sensitivity coefficients, Θ_{ij}, are shown explicitly.

$$S = \pm[\Sigma\Sigma(\Theta_{ij})^2(S_{ij})^2]^{1/2} \tag{6-9}$$

Recall that for both Eqs. (3-3) and (6-9), Eq. (3-2) applies. That is,

$$S_{ij} = \pm[s_{ij}/(N_{ij})^{1/2}]$$

Extending Eq. (6-9) to the case of weighted precision, the following formula is obtained:

$$\underline{\underline{S}} = [\Sigma\Sigma(W_{ij})^2(\Theta_{ij})^2(S_{ij})^2]^{1/2} \tag{6-10}$$

Eq. (6-10) is the expression that is used to compute the weighted precision index to be associated with the weighted test result. The weighted precision index is $\underline{\underline{S}}$.

Once the weighted precision index is obtained, it is necessary to compute the weighted degrees of freedom.

Weighted Degrees of Freedom

The standard Welch-Satterthwaite formula for degrees of freedom assignable to a combined precision index is Eq. (3-4):

$$\nu = \frac{[\Sigma\Sigma(S_{ij})^2]^2}{\{\Sigma\Sigma[(S_{ij})^4/\nu_{ij}]\}}$$

The weighted degrees of freedom is obtained by expanding Equation (3-4):

$$\underline{\underline{\nu}} = \frac{[\Sigma\Sigma(W_{ij})^2(\Theta_{ij})^2(S_{ij})^2]^2}{\{\Sigma\Sigma[(W_{ij})^4(\Theta_{ij})^4(S_{ij})^4/\nu_{ij}]\}} \tag{6-11}$$

Note that in Eq. (6-11) the sensitivity coefficients, Θ_{ij}, are shown explicitly along with the weighting factors, W_{ij}. The weighted degrees of freedom is $\underline{\underline{\nu}}$.

Uncertainty, Standard and Weighted

The standard uncertainty interval was given in Section 3-4 for the U_{ADD} model and the U_{RSS} model. They were Eqs. (3-10) and (3-14), respectively, shown as

$$U_{ADD} = \pm[B + t_{95}S]$$

and

$$U_{RSS} = \pm[(B)^2 + (t_{95}S)^2]^{1/2}$$

The corresponding weighted uncertainty intervals, $\underline{U}_{ADD}$ and $\underline{U}_{RSS}$, are:

$$\underline{U}_{ADD} = \pm[\underline{B} + t_{95}\underline{S}] \tag{6-12}$$
$$\underline{U}_{RSS} = \pm[(\underline{B})^2 + (t_{95}\underline{S})^2]^{1/2} \tag{6-13}$$

Eqs. (6-12) and (6-13) represent the weighted uncertainty that should be computed for any weighted test result.

Example 6-1:
For the simple case of two nondependent measurement methods, the following is assumed:

1. All influence coefficients are unity; the errors are in result units.
2. The critical data for the two methods are as follows:

Method	Result	B	S	ν	U_{ADD}
A	5.0 psia	±0.5	±0.3	15	±1.14
B	7.0 psia	±0.3	±0.1	12	±0.58

Using Eq. 6-1, the standard average is obtained:

$$\overline{X} = [(16)(5.0) + (13)(7.0)]/(16 + 13) = 5.90 \text{ psia}$$

Using Eq. (6-2), the weighted average is obtained. But first, the weights must be obtained. They are calculated with Eq. (6-3):

$$W_A = (1/1.14)^2/[(1/1.14)^2 + (1/0.58)^2] = 0.206$$
$$W_B = (1/0.58)^2/[(1/1.14)^2 + (1/0.58)^2] = 0.794$$

Note that W_A plus W_B equals 1.000. This is a good check on the correct calculation of the weighting factors.

The weighted average may now be calculated using Eq. (6-2).

$$\underline{\underline{X}} = (0.206)(5.0) + (0.794)(7.0) = 6.6 \text{ psia}$$

This is the best answer or test result that can be obtained with the measurements given.

The weighted uncertainty may now be calculated. First, the weighted bias is calculated with Eq. (6-8):

$$\underline{\underline{B}} = \pm[(0.206)^2(1.0)^2(0.5)^2 + (0.794)^2(1.0)^2(0.3)^2]^{1/2} = \pm 0.26$$

The weighted precision index may now be calculated with Eq. (6-10):

$$\underline{\underline{S}} = \pm[(0.206)^2(1.0)^2(0.3)^2 + (0.794)^2(1.0)^2(0.1)^2]^{1/2} = \pm 0.10$$

The weighted degrees of freedom are calculated with Eq. (6-11):

$$\underline{\underline{\nu}} = \frac{\pm\{[(0.206)^2(1.0)^2(0.3)^2 + (0.794)^2(1.0)^2(0.1)^2]^2}{[(0.26)^4(1.0)^4(0.3)^4/15 + (0.794)^4(1.0)^4(0.1)^4/12]\}}$$

$$= \pm\{(0.10)^4/(0.00000428)\} = 23.4 = 23$$

The weighted uncertainty is then calculated using Eq. (6-12):

$$\underline{\underline{U}} = \pm[0.26 + (2.069)(0.10)] = \pm 0.47$$

Note that a weighted uncertainty of ± 0.47 is better than the best single measurement uncertainty of ± 0.58. Weighting works!!

References

1. Dieck, R. H., "I made that one up myself," 1987.
2. Brownlee, K. A., *Statistical Theory and Methodology in Science and Engineering*, pp 72–74, (John Wiley & Sons, 1960).
3. ANSI/ASME PTC 19.1-1985, *Instruments and Apparatus, Part I, Measurement Uncertainty*, pp 27–28.

Exercises:

6-1. *Why Weight Problem*
    a. *What is the primary reason for calculating a weighted result?*
    b. *What is the units requirement for a weighting computation?*

6-2. Weighting by Uncertainty Problem

Test Method	$\overline{X}$	B	$2S_{\overline{X}}$	ν
1	95°F	±6°F	±2°F	30
2	102°F	±10°F	±3°F	80
3	89°F	±8°F	±9°F	30

a. *Calculate grand average for the methods.*

The weighting formula for W_1 *is:*

$$W_1 = \frac{(1/U_1)^2}{(1/U_1)^2 + (1/U_2)^2 + (1/U_3)^2}$$

$$= \frac{(U_2 U_3)^2}{(U_2 U_3)^2 + (U_1 U_3)^2 + (U_1 U_2)^2}$$

b. *Derive weighting formulae for* W_2 *and* W_3.
c. *Evaluate value of* W_1, W_2, *and* W_3. *How can you check your results here?*
d. *Compute: i. weighted average, X.*
          ii. weighted uncertainty, U_{ADD}, U_{RSS}.
e. *Compare grand average with the weighted average* (X) *and* (U_{ADD} *and* U_{RSS}) *with the average* ($\overline{X}$) *and the smallest* (U_{ADD} *and* U_{RSS}) *above. Why are they different?*

Unit 7:
Applied Considerations

UNIT 7

Applied Considerations

In this unit, several data validation and analysis methods will be presented. These methods are valuable tools for an experimenter working on an uncertainty analysis. The methods are widely known and most are powerful. One or two are widely used but offer very misleading results for the unwary analyst. Often, measurement uncertainty standards and articles assume the experimenter already knows these techniques and how to apply them. Here, each will be presented so an individual new to this type of analysis will be able to use them to improve the quality and applicability of an uncertainty analysis.

Learning Objectives — When you have completed this unit, you should:

   A. Understand how to select the proper units for errors.

   B. Understand the basics of outlier rejection.

   C. Understand the underlying assumptions and proper application of curve fitting techniques.

   D. Have a grasp of the use and weaknesses associated with correlation coefficients.

   E. Know how to test data for normality.

   F. Understand the basics of sampling error, its estimation, and its elimination.

7-1. General Considerations

This unit is a side trip from the path to a valid uncertainty analysis but an important one, since the use of these techniques will often reveal a problem in the test data that would negate the validity of the uncertainty analysis. Having these tools available will often keep the new as well as the experienced analyst out of trouble.

7-2. Choice of Error Units

In previous units, the subject of units has surfaced. It is important to have units that are consistent in every uncertainty analysis formula. In addition, the rule for choice of units is: *choose error units that result in Gaussian-normal error data distributions*. This is the classical "bell-shaped" curve.

The reasons for this rule are: with Gaussian-normal error data, the following are well defined and have well understood meaning:

A. Precision

B. Standard deviation

C. Variance (the square of the standard deviation)

D. Correlation

E. All other statistical terms used in uncertainty analysis

With anything but Gaussian-normal data, the above are not well defined and their use could lead to unrealistic and/or erroneous conclusions.

In addition, as covered in Unit 5, matching units are needed for a viable and correct error propagation.

Method of Units Choice

The following example illustrates a method for proper units choice. Consider Figs. 7-1 and 7-2, which are called *probability plots*. This is a special kind of data plotting covered in Section 7-6 in which Gaussian-normal data plots as a straight line; that is, if the data are normally distributed, they will appear as a straight line on this kind of paper.

It should be noted at this time that your "handy-dandy" local statistician probably has a computer program to both make these plots and to test the normality of data without plotting using a standard statistical test such as Bartlett's Test (1). This plotting technique is recommended for most analysis efforts since the results can be seen and are thus more easily understood.

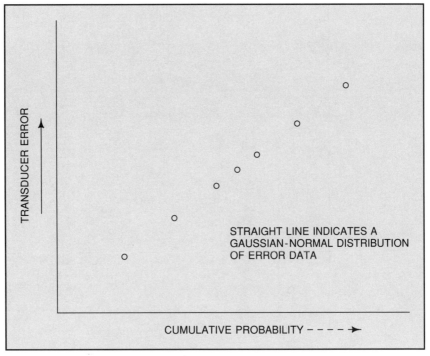

Fig. 7-1. Probability Plot of Pressure Transducer Error Data in % Full-Scale Units

Returning to Figs. 7-1 and 7-2, it is noted that the percent full-scale error data in Fig. 7-1 are a straight line, indicating the errors are normally distributed. This means that the data is Gaussian-normal. This is the kind of data that should be used in an error analysis. Fig. 7-2 illustrates the same exact error data but transformed into percent of reading. The data in Fig. 7-2 are not normally distributed. This data is not to be used in uncertainty analysis.

The only difference between the data plotted in Fig. 7-1 and Fig. 7-2 is a transformation of the same error data. It is easy to convert this data from one to the other, which is usually the case with other error data as well. For pressure transducers, usually the proper error data is percent full-scale units, or absolute units, e.g., ± 0.13 psi. Percent full-scale units are the same as absolute units divided by the full-scale absolute value.

Other instrument types are properly expressed as percent of reading units, such as turbine flowmeter error data and thermocouple error data.

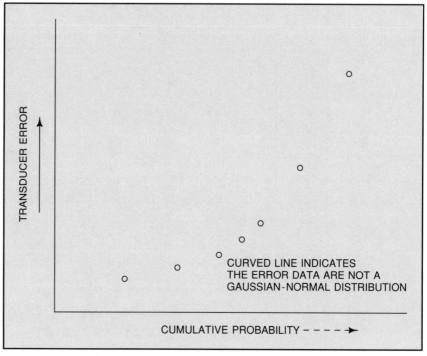

Fig. 7-2. Probability Plot of Pressure Transducer Error Data, % Reading Units

Summary of Units

In summary, the proper units are needed for a correct error analysis. They are needed for error propagation and all the uncertainty analysis formulas. Several choices are available. The most common are percent of point or percent of level, percent full scale or absolute, or some combination. Care is needed to be sure that the units chosen result in the error data being Gaussian-normally distributed.

7-3. Treatment of Outliers

Definitions and Opinions

First of all, how is an outlier defined? Several definitions are available.

    A. Outlier data is spurious data.

    B. Outlier data is the same as wild points (whatever that means).

C. Outlier data is unexplained data.

D. Outlier data is data that disproves my thesis (this is my favorite definition).

This author eschews rejecting any data from a set as an outlier. There are two primary reasons for this position:

A. Outlier rejection is biased in the philosophical sense. That is, when did an experimenter ever reject a data point in order to better *disprove* the point being made? Think about it. Never, right? Outlier rejection is always used to better *prove* a point or to make a data set *look* better. It is biased toward making a data set better prove the thesis or postulate. This kind of action should always be avoided if possible.

B. The second reason this author *loathes* outlier rejection is that it is a poor way to improve data sets. If rejecting an outlier changes the conclusion of an experiment or set of measurements, a better set of data is needed. It is inappropriate for the conclusion(s) to rest on one data point.

Outlier Rejection Methods

Outlier data, therefore, should not be rejected. However, since it is human nature to make things look better, the following technique is given so that at least the approach to outlier rejection is objective. It is important to have an objective method for such rejection. There are two such common methods: Grubbs' Technique (1) and Thompson's tau (τ) (2).

Grubbs' Technique for outlier rejection is largely a 3σ technique. In essence, it rejects all data more than 3σ from the average. It seldom rejects good data (data within normal data scatter). Grubbs' Technique rejects few data points.

Thompson's tau (τ) is more a 2σ technique. It sometimes will reject good data (data within normal scatter).

The outlier rejection method recommended herein is Thompson's tau (τ).

Outlier Rejection Cautions

It should be noted that several outlier rejection rules apply for the prudent analyst:

A. Reject outliers only with caution.

B. Never reject outliers by judgment (subjectively).

C. Reject outliers only analytically (objectively).

Outlier Rejection Recommended Procedure, Thompson's tau (τ)

Consider the Table 7-1 of error data.

Note that, by observation, -555 may be an outlier. To determine whether or not it is, Thompson's τ technique should be applied as follows.

Step 1. Calculate the data set average, $\overline{X}$, and the standard deviation, S_X; note the number of data points, 40 in this case.

Here, $\overline{X} = 1.125$ and $S_X = 140.8$.

Step 2. Note the suspected outlier, -555.

Step 3. Calculate delta, $\delta = |(\text{suspect outlier}) - (\overline{X})|$, (absolute value).

Here, $\delta = |(-555) - (1.125)| = 556.125$.

Step 4. Obtain the Thompson's tau (τ) from the table in Appendix E.

Here, $\tau = 1.924$.

26	79	58	24	1	−103	−121	−220
−11	−137	120	124	129	−38	25	−60
148	−52	−216	12	−56	89	8	−29
−107	20	9	−40	0	2	10	166
126	−72	179	41	127	−35	334	−555

Table 7-1. Sample of Error Data

Step 5. Calculate the product of τ and S_X.

Here, $\tau S_X = (1.924) * (140.8) = 270.9$.

Step 6. Compare δ with τS_X. If δ is $> \tau S_X$, X is an outlier. If δ is $< \tau S_X$, then X is not an outlier.

Here, that is, $556.125 > 270.9$; therefore, -555 is an outlier.

Step 7. Now search for the next most likely outlier. Recompute the average, $\overline{X}$, and the standard deviation, S_X; follow through with steps 2 through 6.

Step 8. This process is repeated until a suspected outlier yields a δ that is $< \tau S_X$. When the last X data point checked is not a outlier and the process stops.

Outlier Rejection Caution

This method for identifying outliers is to be used with caution. For the reasons cited previously, outlier rejection is to be done only with care. In addition, Thompson's τ will often identify valid data for rejection. For this reason as well, this outlier rejection method should be used to identify *possible* outliers for elimination from the data set should a good reason *also* be found. It is not advisable to eliminate outliers just to make the data set "look nice."

7-4. Curve Fitting

General Comments

It has been said that "the use of polynomial curve fits is an admission of ignorance" (3). Most experimenters have used curve fitting routines to better present their data and to better understand the physical phenomena under investigation. However, the statistical assumptions underlying the use of curve fitting algorithms now available are often ignored if, in fact, the experimenter knows about them.

Curve fitting routines available on modern computers are powerful tools that should be used with caution. They all have many underlying assumptions.

The foremost curve fitting method available is that of least-squares (4). It will be the method presented in this ILM.

Basic Assumptions of Least-Squares Curve Fitting

Least-squares curve fitting methods have the following major statistically based assumptions:

A. The curve being fitted is continuous in the region of interest.

B. The curve being fitted has a continuous first derivative in the region of interest.

C. Over the range of interest, there is equal risk of error in the data.

The first two assumptions are statisticalese, are very common in the world of the mathematician and statistician, and have little use for the uncertainty analyst. It is assumed that these first two assumptions will never be violated in experimental or test data sets.

The third assumption is often violated by scientists, engineers, and experimenters. It means that when the curve is fit, there is equal risk of error in the data around the curve. That is, the data scatter looks the same across the whole range of the data of interest. Figs. 7-3 and 7-4 illustrate this point.

Fig. 7-3 shows a data set in which the scatter around the curve fit is the same across the whole range of the curve. This is equal risk of error. It is the result to which all curve fitting people should aspire.

Fig. 7-4 shows a curve fit in which the data scatter is larger at the lower end than at the higher end of the curve. This is NOT equal risk of error. The basic underlying assumptions of statistics have been violated and the curve fit should not be used. This curve fit is typical of the plot of nozzle calibrations. At the high flows and Reynolds numbers, the data scatter is usually small, a testimony to the precision of the pressure transducers that measure the delta pressure across the nozzle. At the low flows and Reynolds numbers, there is considerable scatter in excess of that at the high end. This, too, is typical of the results obtained with typical pressure transducers on a

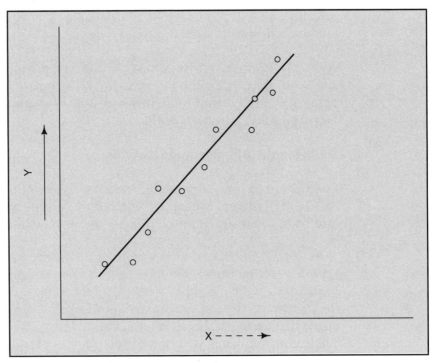

Fig. 7-3. Curve Fit of Data with Equal Risk of Error

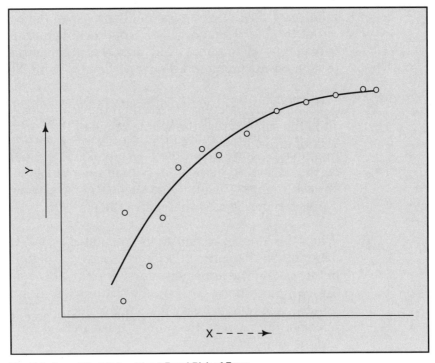

Fig. 7-4. Curve Fit of Data without Equal Risk of Error

nozzle. This kind of curve fit is anathema. The competent analyst will never use it.

A note of interest, when curve fits of the type shown in Fig. 7-4 show up, they can often be corrected by a transformation of the data, possibly to semi-log. However, these transformations can be very tricky, so watch out!

Additional Guidance and Cautions

In addition to the fundamental statistical assumptions behind valid curve fitting, here are a number of helpful hints this author has learned to heed over his many years of mistakes.

   A. *Avoid the use of polynomial curve fitting wherever possible.* As mentioned before, its use is an admission of ignorance. Note: *"Stupid is forever, ignorance can be fixed."* (5) Of what is the experimenter ignorant when polynomial curve fits are used? He is not stupid, certainly, just ignorant. The experimenter is ignorant of the physics of the problem. The physical form is not known. The theoretical relationship is not known.

This may be stated another way: *Use the theoretical relationship wherever possible.* It will keep the experimenter out of trouble. The most likely spot for this trouble is the space between the data points. This fact is also related to the number of data points fitted and the type of curve being fit.

   B. *The number of constants calculated in a curve fit should be much less than the number of data points* (6). Every curve fit computes a number of constants. These constants may be for the physical form or for the polynomial. The number of constants should be much less than the number of data points or vast trouble will surely be encountered between the data points when one attempts to use the curve fit.

When the number of constants calculated equals the number of data points, the curve fit will go exactly through each data point, giving the appearance of a fine fit. However, to go through those points, gigantic gyrations will occur between the points. Since the primary use for any curve fit is to extract information between the points, this can be devastating to any serious analysis.

More on the real problems of violating hints A and B later.

C. *2SEE for curve fits is analogous to* $2S_X$ *for data.* $2S_X$ for data is an expression and description of the scatter of the data around a biased average. (Remember that all averages are biased from the true value, and an important part of any uncertainty analysis is to estimate that bias. It cannot be seen in the data as the effects of precision error sources can.)

SEE stands for *Standard Estimate of Error*. It is a description and estimation of the scatter of the data about a fitted line or curve. The formulas for S_X and SEE are comparable. Note Eqs. (2-3) and (7-1):

$$S_X = \pm\{[\Sigma(X_i - \overline{X})^2/(n - 1)]^{1/2}\} \qquad (2\text{-}3)$$

$$SEE = \pm\{[\Sigma(Y_i - Y_{ci})^2/(n - K)]^{1/2}\} \qquad (7\text{-}1)$$

where for both:

n = the number of data points in the S_X or the fit
K = the number of constants in the fit
$\overline{X}$ = the data set average
X_i = the ith data point in the data set or fit
Y_{ci} = the Y calculated at X_i from the curve fit
Y_i = the ith measurement of Y in the fit
$n - 1$ = the degrees of freedom associated with S_X
$n - K$ = the degrees of freedom for the curve fit.

Note that both equations have exactly the same form. Both S_X (the generic form of s_{ij}, the standard deviation of the data) and SEE are expressions of the scatter of the data. S_X is scatter about the average, and SEE is scatter about the fitted curve or line.

D. *A low SEE is not necessarily an indicator of a good curve fit. Corollary: For multiple polynomial curve fits, the one with the lowest SEE is not necessarily the best curve fit to use.* A low $2S_X$ is indicative of a low precision error in the experiment. It is often thought that a low 2SEE is indicative of an accurate (or the best) curve fit. One can get into trouble with that assumption, as can be seen in Table 7-2.

When observing the 2SEE values in Table 7-2, it could be assumed that the lowest 2SEE would be indicative of the best curve fit, the one that should be used by the experimenter. FEW THINGS could be further from the truth. The lowest 2SEE is for curve fit order 5; it is actually the worst curve fit! (This will be illustrated in Fig. 7-5.) Its use also ignores hint A: Use

Fit Order	2SEE in %CO_2
1	0.194
2	0.052
3	0.058
4	0.039
5	0.007

Table 7-2. Comparison of 2SEE Obtained for Several CO_2 Curve Fit Orders

theoretical relationships wherever possible and avoid polynomial curve fits wherever possible.

F. *The 2SEE of a curve fit should approximate the error in the standards used in the calibration.* It is not reasonable to have less data scatter about a curve fit than the comparative scatter in the calibration standards. This is illustrated in the next section.

Example of Curve Fitting Problems

The problems covered in hints A through D are all illustrated in Fig. 7-5. That figure presents CO_2 calibration data and its several curve fits to show that polynomial curve fits can cause problems, that the number of constants calculated should be less than the number of data points, that SEE is analogous to S_X, and that the lowest 2SEE is not necessarily an indicator of the best curve fit.

Fig. 7-5 presents several curve fits. Polynomial curve fits for 2nd, 3rd, 4th and 5th order are shown for CO_2 analyzer calibration data consisting of seven data points. Also shown is the manufacturer's recommended curve form, an exponential.

Note that in Fig. 7-5 the second, third, fourth, and fifth order curve fits that are illustrated are the curve fits whose 2SEE values are listed in Table 7-2. See how badly the fifth-order curve fits the proper shape for this exponential instrument. Particularly between 0.0 and 0.6% CO_2, substantial between-point errors are encountered when using the curve. This is the reason the fit should have many less constants calculated than the number of data points available for fitting.

The next question is: "What is a fit order that is 'much less' than the number of data points?" First realize that "fit order" applies only to polynomial curve fits. What is intended by the

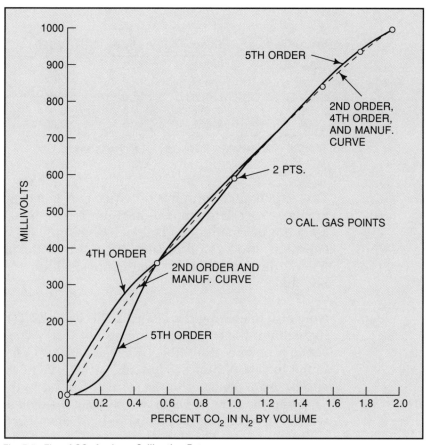

Fig. 7-5. Fits of CO$_2$ Analyzer Calibration Data

question is: "What is a number of constants that is 'much less' than the number of data points in the fit?"

Observe in Fig. 7-5 that there are 7 data points. Obviously (meaning even I can see), a fifth-order fit with six constants is not "much less" than the number of data points. How about fourth order (five constants)? That is also no good. Substantial between-point errors are still encountered when using the curve. However, second order appears really good. In fact, it overlays the manufacturer's exponential curve. Second order has three constants, less than half the number of data points. This would seem a good start. *The curve fit should have at least twice the number of data points as the number of constants calculated in the fit.* In the case of the second-order fit, another curve fit was also tried—an exponential of the form:

$$Y = Ae^{bX} \tag{7-2}$$

Instrument	Range	Fit Order	%CO$_2$ 2SEE	(Standard) Cal. Gas Error %CO$_2$
CO$_2$—A	0–5%	3	0.028	0.044
	0–2%	3	0.020	0.022
CO$_2$—B	0–18%	6	0.101	0.115
	0–5%	6	0.035	0.044
	0–2%	5	0.0073	0.022

Table 7-3. CO$_2$ Instrument Polynomial Calibration Curves

This exponential form has only two constants and was the best fit since it overlaid the manufacturer's curve and the simple second order mentioned before. This simple fit, with two constants, did so well because it is actually the physical form. It conforms with hint A: Use the physical form whenever possible.

Note also that using the lowest 2SEE value in Table 7-2 as an indicator of the best curve fit does not work. The best fit was actually second order. Its 2SEE was 0.052% CO$_2$. This brings us to the impact of hint F: The 2SEE of a curve fit should approximate the error in the standards used in the calibration. Consider the data in Table 7-3. Review the data and consider which curve fits are proper and which are "over fits" of the calibration data. This will be left as an exercise for the student.

Least-Squares Curve Fitting

Since it is important to use curve fits that match the physical form wherever possible, it is important to know how to do a least-squares fit on an equation. Most least-squares curve fits are done on polynomials, and the illustrations in this unit will be on polynomials. However, it should be clearly noted that these methods will apply to other forms as well, as for example, a simple exponential given as Eq. (7-2).

In this section, the basics of least-squares curve fitting will be presented. The fit illustrated will be that of a straight line. Consider Fig. 7-6. The form for a straight line is:

$$Y = aX + b \qquad (7\text{-}3)$$

Note in Fig. 7-6 that epsilon (ϵ) is also shown. ϵ is used to represent the error between the line fit and the data points.

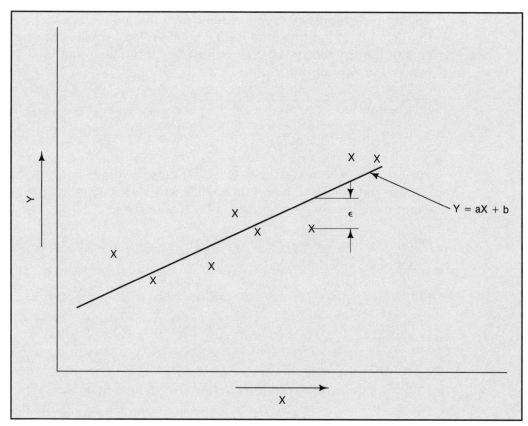

Fig. 7-6. Least-Squares Line Fit

$$\epsilon = Y - (aX + b) \qquad (7\text{-}4)$$

To derive the least-squares equations for the straight line fit, the following process is used.

The line form is:

$$Y = aX + b$$

For one point *on* the line, the following is true:

$$Y_i = aX_i + b \qquad (7\text{-}5)$$

For one point *off* the line, the following is true:

$$Y_i = aX_i + b + \epsilon_{Y_i} \qquad (7\text{-}6)$$

The term ϵ_{Y_i} represents the error between the point (X_i, Y_i) and the Y_i value of the line fit at X_i. To obtain a least-squares fit, the sum of the squares of these ϵ_{Y_i}'s must be minimized; that is, it is necessary to minimize $\Sigma [(\epsilon_{Y_i})^2]$.

It is noted that

$$\Sigma[(\epsilon_{Y_i})^2] = \Sigma[(Y_i - aX_i - b)^2] \qquad (7\text{-}7)$$

For $\Sigma[(\epsilon_{Y_i})^2]$ to be minimized, Eq. (7-7) must be differentiated with respect to a and b and those differentials set equal to zero. a and b are the floating constants for this curve fit.

Differentiating the square of Eq. (7-7) and setting the results equal to zero, the following are obtained:

$$(\partial/\partial a)[\Sigma(Y_i^2 + a^2X_i^2 + b^2 - 2Y_iaX_i - 2Y_ib + 2abX_i)] = 0.0$$
$$(7\text{-}8)$$
$$(\partial/\partial b)[\Sigma(Y_i^2 + a^2X_i^2 + b^2 - 2Y_iaX_i - 2Y_ib + 2abX_i)] = 0.0$$
$$(7\text{-}9)$$

Dropping noninvolved terms, the following are obtained:

$$(\partial/\partial a)[\Sigma(a^2X_i^2) - 2\Sigma(Y_iaX_i) + 2\Sigma(abX_i)] = 0.0 \qquad (7\text{-}10)$$
$$(\partial/\partial a)[\Sigma(b^2) - 2\Sigma(Y_ib) + 2\Sigma(abX_i)] = 0.0 \qquad (7\text{-}11)$$

The resulting simultaneous equations are:

$$0 = 2a\Sigma X_i^2 - 2\Sigma Y_iX_i + 2b\Sigma X_i \qquad (7\text{-}12)$$
$$= 2\Sigma b - 2\Sigma Y_i + 2a\Sigma X_i$$
$$= 2nb - 2\Sigma Y_i + 2a\Sigma X_i \qquad (7\text{-}13)$$

Working through the algebra, the solutions for a and b are obtained.

From Eq. (7-12).

$$b = [\Sigma(Y_iX_i) - a\Sigma(X_i)^2]/[\Sigma(X_i)] \qquad (7\text{-}14)$$

By substitution into Eq. (7-13) and rearranging, the solution for the constant a is obtained.

$$a = [[n\Sigma(Y_iX_i) - \Sigma(X_i)\Sigma(Y_i)]/\{[n\Sigma(X_i)^2] - [\Sigma(X_i)]^2\}] \qquad (7\text{-}15)$$

Substituting Eq. (7-15) into Eq. (7-14) and reorganizing, the solution for constant b is obtained.

$$b = \Sigma(Y_i)/n - a\Sigma(X_i)/n = \overline{Y} - a\overline{X} \qquad (7\text{-}16)$$

The application of these principles is covered in the exercises.

7-5. Correlation Coefficients, Their Use and Misuse

General Comments

Probably one of the most misunderstood and misused statistics is the correlation coefficient. It is valuable in uncertainty analysis because it is an indicator of relationship. It is needed for uncertainty analysis when errors are not completely independent, as covered in Section 5-3.

However, although an indicator, it is not proof of cause and effect. This is the point on which most experimenters and novice uncertainty analysts find themselves frequently impaled. *Correlation is not necessarily demonstration of cause and effect.* This fact is hard to believe for some but, as proof, consider this situation: If one were to calculate a correlation coefficient between the price of haircuts in New York City and the population of Puerto Rico, a strong correlation would be obtained; that is, the correlation coefficient would be near one. Since correlation coefficients can be only in the range of -1.0 to $+1.0$, one would think that getting a correlation coefficient near $+1.0$ would indicate relationship and/or cause and effect. However, as can be intuitively seen, there is no cause and effect between the population of Puerto Rico and the price of haircuts in New York City. There is relationship but not cause and effect.

The Correlation Coefficient

The correlation coefficient for an infinite data set, or the whole population, is ρ; for a data sample, it is r. In uncertainty analysis, as with the calculation of S_X or the choice of σ, one seldom has the whole population and must calculate r, not ρ, just as one calculates S_X and not σ. The formula for the correlation coefficient for the data sample is, therefore:

$$r_{XY} = \frac{n\Sigma(X_i Y_i) - (\Sigma X_i)(\Sigma Y_i)}{\{[n\Sigma(X_i^2) - (\Sigma X_i)^2][n\Sigma(Y_i^2) - (\Sigma Y_i)^2]\}^{1/2}} \qquad (7\text{-}17)$$

Eq. (7-17) looks like an easy visit to your calculator, but it is not. It is worth calculating r once for training purposes; after that, do it with a programmable calculator or a computer.

Correlation Coefficient as an Estimator of Explained Variance

The correlation coefficient squared, r^2, is often used as an estimation of the variance in one error source that is explained by the second. That is, Eq. (7-18) can be used in uncertainty analysis to decide how much variance in one variable, $(S_X)^2$, may be explained by variance in the second correlated error source variance, $(S_Y)^2$.

$$(r_{XY}^2) = \frac{\text{(explained variation)}}{\text{(total variation)}} \qquad (7\text{-}18)$$

Although Eq. (7-18) is true, it is not often needed in uncertainty analysis. It is useful at times, however.

The Significant Correlation Coefficient

Prior to using the calculated correlation coefficient in an uncertainty analysis where some error sources are nonindependent, it is necessary to determine whether or not the calculated correlation coefficient is significant in the statistical sense. Although many statistics texts have analytical tests for this evaluation, a graphical approach is often used for simplicity. Consider Figs. 7-7 and 7-8.

After calculating r, the sample correlation coefficient, it is necessary to know that the possible range for ρ, the population correlation coefficient, does not contain 0.0. If the range for the population coefficient includes 0.0, it is not possible to know with a stated confidence that the sample correlation coefficient, r, is significantly different from 0.0.

A correlation coefficient of 0.0 indicates there is no evidence that the error sources are correlated. Similarly, if the range of the population correlation coefficient, ρ, includes 0.0, it is not possible to state that correlation has been established.

To determine the significance of the sample correlation coefficient, r, the two curves of Figs. 7-7 and 7-8 may be used. The procedure is as follows.

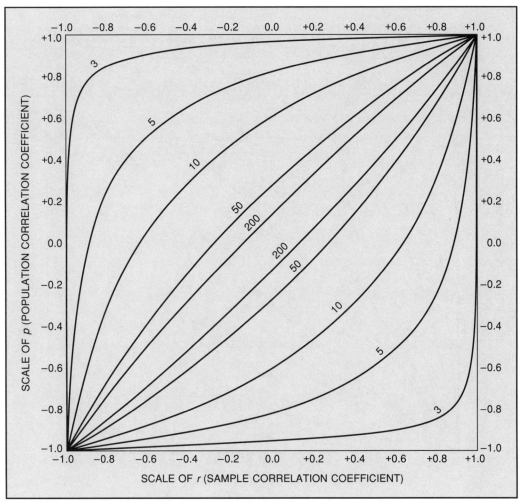

Fig. 7-7. 95% Confidence Interval on r (Reference 10)

After calculating the sample correlation coefficient, r, and noting the number of data points in the calculation, one may check to be sure with 95% confidence that the correlation coefficient is non-zero with Fig. 7-7. Merely enter Fig. 7-7 at the horizontal axis with the calculated sample correlation coefficient. Read up the figure until the line delineating the sample size is met; then proceed to the left to obtain the lower limit for the population correlation coefficient, ρ^-. Continue up the vertical line for the sample correlation coefficient until the line delineating the sample size is again met; read to the left to obtain the upper limit for the population correlation coefficient,

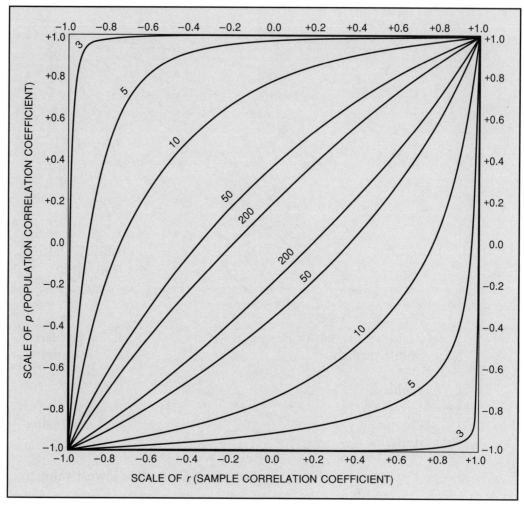

Fig. 7-8. 99% Confidence Interval on r (Reference 10)

ρ^+. One then has the following:

$$\rho^- \le r \le \rho^+ \tag{7-19}$$

As long as the range illustrated in Eq. (7-19) does not contain zero, the population correlation coefficient is non-zero to 95% confidence; the sample correlation coefficient, r, is significant and should be used in error propagation for nonindependent variables.

Similarly for 99% confidence, use the curves in Fig. 7-8. The 95% confidence test is the recommended approach.

7-6. Tests for Normality, Probability Plots

General Comments

In all the combinations of standard deviation mentioned in this ILM, there has been the implicit assumption that the data sampled is normally distributed. It is appropriate to test for this normality.

A quantitative test for normality is the Kolmogorov-Smirnov Test Statistic (7). This and other tests provide fine quantitative answers to the question of normality.

However, it is often more instructive to the uncertainty analyst to use a more qualitative technique called probability plotting. A detailed explanation of probability plotting is given in Reference 7 and is covered with clear illustrations in J. R. King's book (9).

Besides the clear indication of normality, much can be learned from a probability plot of the error data, as will now be seen.

Probability Plotting Procedure

The procedure for making probability plots has the following steps.

Step 1. Arrange the data in an increasing list, lowest value to highest.

Step 2. Assign ''median ranks'' to each numbered data point using Benard's formula (9) following:

$$P_{0.50} = (i - 0.3)/(N + 0.4) \qquad (7\text{-}20)$$

where:

$P_{0.50}$ = the 50% median rank
i = the number of the ordered data points being plotted
N = the number of data points plotted

Step 3. Plot the data against its median rank (or cumulative percent, which is the median rank times 100) on normal probability paper. *Any of several kinds of normal probability paper are available.*

Step 4. Observe the shape of the curve plotted and decide if it is sufficiently close to a straight line to be considered normally distributed data. Data that is a straight line on this special paper is normally distributed.

Alternate Method for Probability Plotting (without Special Paper)

If the special paper is not available, an identical plot of the data can be made by altering step 3 above as follows:

Step 3. After assigning median ranks, determine from the table in Appendix F the equivalent fraction of sigma, σ, associated with that median rank. (Interpolate the table in Appendix F linearly for adequate precision.) Then plot the data set, in order, against its sigma fraction, σ, on rectilinear graph paper. The resulting curve shapes will be identical to those obtained with the special probability paper.

Then proceed with step 4 as shown.

Additional Information in Probability Plots

Probability plots offer additional information besides an assessment of data normality:

  A. The slope of the straight line is proportional to the standard deviation of the data.

  B. The 50% point is the average of the data set.

To determine the data set standard deviation, find the 50% and 2.5% points on the Y axis, subtract them, and divide by 2; this difference is the S_X interval.

To determine data set average, just read the vertical axis at the point where the straight line of the data goes through the 50% point (or the 0.0 σ point if plotting against σ has been done because probability plotting paper was not available).

Examples of Probability Plots

When data is plotted on probability paper, the shapes of the curves are often most informative. When they are straight lines,

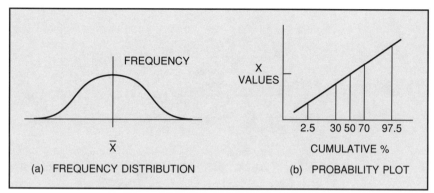

Fig. 7-9. Normal Distribution

the data is normally distributed. When there are curve shapes other than a straight line, the shapes themselves are revealing.

Consider Figs. 7-9(a) and (b). Fig. 7-9(a) is the typical plot of a normal distribution. When such a data set is plotted on probability paper, Fig. 7-9(b) results. It is a straight line, indicating the data set is normally distributed.

Now consider Figs. 7-10(a) and (b). Figure 7-10(a) is a typical plot of a data set in which two normal distributions are included in the set, but their averages are different and there is no overlap of the data. This is often called a bimodal distribution. Note: In Fig. 7-10,(b) is the probability plot of the data in Fig. 7-10(a); there are two separate straight lines. This indicates two distributions in one data set. It might be thought that Fig. 7-10(b) is unnecessary since one can see the bimodality in Fig. 7-10(a). However, a real data set is not so neatly separated as shown in Figure 7-10(a). Fig. 7-10(b)

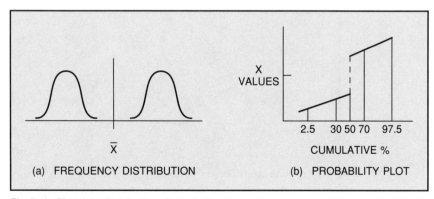

Fig. 7-10. Bimodular Distributions Separated

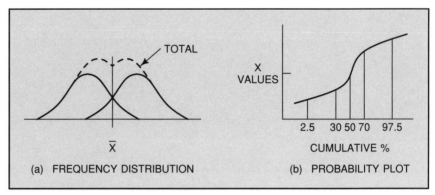

Fig. 7-11. Bimodular Distributions Overlapped

separates it neatly. Here, the bimodular data has been separated into two straight lines, each with its own average and standard deviation.

Now consider the data in Figs. 7-11(a) and (b). Here the bimodular data exists in two distributions that overlap. When this happens, as in Fig. 7-11(a), the probability plot will look like the data in Fig. 7-11(b), that is, an "S" shape.

Look at the data plotted in Figs. 7-12(a) and (b). Two frequency distributions of data are plotted in Fig. 7-12(a). They are not bimodular but nested. The probability plot of Fig. 7-12(b) shows this by having a reverse "S" curve. It is the inverse "S" as compared to Fig. 7-11(b) for bimodular data.

Finally, consider the data in Fig. 7-13. Actual differences obtained by comparing two CO_2 instruments on the same process stream have been probability plotted.

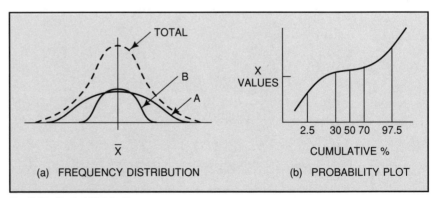

Fig. 7-12. Nested Distributions

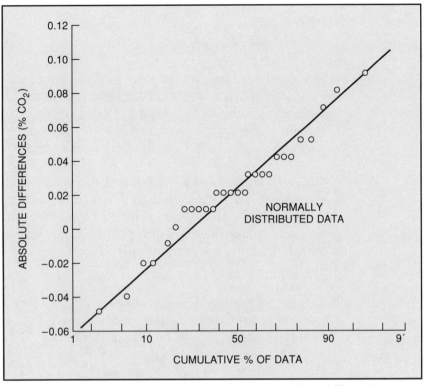

Fig. 7-13. Probability Plot of Absolute Differences between Two Individual CO$_2$ Analyzers

At first it appears to be normally distributed; that is, if S were calculated, it could be properly used because the data are normally distributed. However, note also that the data is stacked up every 0.01% CO$_2$. This is called a "least-count" problem; it indicates that the instruments used to compute these delta CO$_2$ readings could not yield data with any finer increments than 0.01% CO$_2$. This is not usually a problem in uncertainty analysis except to note that the problem exists and that it would be unreasonable to try to measure a difference smaller than 0.01% CO$_2$.

7-7. Sampling Error

Special Considerations

Sampling error is often misunderstood by the novice uncertainty analyst. It can be used to represent any of three (or more) error types or sources. The most common three are:

  A. variation in space,

B. variation in time, and

C. sampling error.

The most common uncertainty analysis problem is when *real variation is misunderstood to be random error*. This real variation can be real variation in space or time. True sampling error is *the residual random error after accounting for all the real effects, such as those of space and/or time*.

One way to evaluate the effects of space and/or time is to see your local statistician and have him or her run an analysis of variance on your test data. The problems with this approach are that most experimenters don't understand what is happening and that results are evident only after the completion of the analysis.

This section presents a simplified analysis of variance technique sometimes called "matrix analysis." This matrix analysis technique will be first presented in all the gory detail of the full analytical equations. It will then be applied to a simple example so that the student may more clearly understand what is happening.

Gory Detail Analytical Equations, Method

1. Given:

    A. Data (measurements) at a set of spatial locations such as in a pipe or a duct.

    B. Several data acquisitions of the data at each location but spaced in time. It is assumed that all the locations are sampled at the same time but all are sampled several times.

2. The operating equation is defined as follows:

$$\text{Data acquired} = D_{lt} \qquad (7\text{-}21)$$

where:

    D = the actual data point measurement
    l = the location of the measurement in the duct
    t = the time of the measurement (this is the time at which all the data are recorded at all locations)

3. The next step is to obtain the average at each time for across all locations. This is defined by Eq. (7-22).

$$A_t = \sum_{l=1}^{n} (D_{lt})/n \qquad (7\text{-}22)$$

where:

A_t = average of all data at time, t, across all locations, l

n = the number of locations, l

4. It may now be observed, by considering the averages and their times, whether or not there is an effect of change in time. This is something that cannot be seen during an analysis of variance but can be seen here.

5. Next, obtain the differences (δ) by comparing the data at each location to the average at that time, that is,

$$\delta_{lt} = D_{lt} - A_t \qquad (7\text{-}23)$$

where δ_{lt} = the difference between the data at each location, l, and its time, t, average.

6. Now it is necessary to obtain the average of the differences, δ_{lt}, at each location across time, that is,

$$\bar{\delta}_l = \sum_{t=1}^{M} (\delta_{lt})/M \qquad (7\text{-}24)$$

where:

$\bar{\delta}_l$ = the average of all δ_{lt} at location, l, across time, t

M = the number of times averaged

7. Next it is necessary to obtain the differences, Δ, comparing each time difference, δ_{lt}, to its average at location, l, as shown in Eq. (7-25).

$$\Delta_{lt} = \delta_{lt} - \bar{\delta}_l \qquad (7\text{-}25)$$

8. Note that the Δ_{lt} values are the residual errors after the linear variation in time and space are averaged out.

9. The next step is to calculate the sampling error, S_X, using Eq. (7-26).

$$S_X = \pm\{[\Sigma\Sigma(\Delta_{lt} - \overline{\Delta})^2]/[(l - 1)(t - 1)]\}^{1/2} \qquad (7\text{-}26)$$

where $\overline{\Delta} = (\Sigma\Sigma\Delta_{lt})/(l*t)$.

10. It is important to note that the sampling error thus calculated, S_X, should be treated as a precision error source.

It is much easier to understand the calculation of sampling error using the matrix analysis approach when the calculation is presented in real data. Therefore, use the previous section to define the equations needed for the calculation and load them into your computer. In order to understand them, however, consider the following analysis.

Example 7-1:
1. Consider the data or measurements that could be obtained with five thermocouples measuring the temperature in a pipe or full duct, as shown in Fig. 7-14.

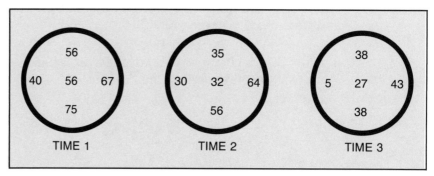

Fig. 7-14. Data for Five Locations' Temperatures and Three Times in a Duct

2. The temperature data can be reorganized in a data matrix of test temperatures, °F, as shown in Table 7-4. Note that the position number need not be rationally assigned to an actual position.

| Times | Locations | | | | |
	1	2	3	4	5
1	56	56	75	40	67
2	35	32	56	30	64
3	38	27	38	5	43

Table 7-4. Pipe Temperature Data Matrix, Location and Time

3. Obtain the average at each time, as shown in Table 7-5.

Times	Locations					Ave. (A_t)
	1	2	3	4	5	
1	56	56	75	40	67	58.8
2	35	32	56	30	64	43.4
3	38	27	38	5	43	30.2

Table 7-5. Pipe Temperature Data Matrix with Time Averages

4. Note that it is possible at this point to observe an effect of time; that is, for later times, the temperature of the fluid in the pipe is lower.

5. Now obtain the differences by comparing each location value to the average at its time.

6. Then obtain the average of those differences at each location across time, as shown in Table 7-6.

Times	Locations					Ave. (A_t)
	1	2	3	4	5	
1	−2.8	−2.8	16.2	−18.8	8.2	58.8
2	−8.4	−11.4	12.6	−13.4	20.6	43.4
3	7.8	−3.2	7.8	−25.2	12.8	30.2
Ave ($\underline{\delta}_{lt}$)	−1.1	−5.8	12.2	−19.1	13.9	

Table 7-6. Pipe Temperature Data Matrix Differences from Time Averages with Location and Time Averages

7. Obtain the differences by comparing each time, δ_{lt}, to its average at location l, $\bar{\delta}_{lt}$, to obtain the residual errors in Table 7-7.

Times	Locations				
	1	2	3	4	5
1	−1.7	3.0	4.0	0.3	−5.7
2	−7.3	−5.6	0.4	5.7	6.7
3	8.9	2.6	−4.4	−6.1	−1.1

Table 7-7. Pipe Temperature Data Matrix with Residual Errors after Removing Linear Effects of Time and Location

8. The values in Table 7-7 are the residual errors after the linear effects of time and location are removed by this "matrix" analysis.

9. $S_X = \pm 6.0°F$. The effect on the average for the pipe is $S_{\bar{X}} = \pm 6.0/\sqrt{8}$, which equals $\pm 2.1°F$.

10. S_X should be treated as another precision error source or elemental precision error, s_{ij}.

Note that the standard deviation of the original data was $S_X = \pm 18.2°F$. There has been a considerable reduction in apparent sampling error through this analysis.

In all the foregoing, it would have been incorrect to have used the variation observed in the pipe as an estimate of the sampling error. $\pm 18.2°F$ was unrealistically high and included the real effects of location and time. The correct answer, or standard deviation for the sampling error, is the $\pm 6.0°F$ just calculated.

References

1. Grubbs, F. E., "Procedures for Detecting Outlying Observations in Samples," *Technometrics*, vol. 11, no. 1, Feb. 1969.
2. Thompson, W. R., "On Criteria for the Rejection of Observations and the Distribution of the Ratio of the Deviations to Sample Standard Deviation," *Annals of Mathematical Statistics*, vol. 6, 1935, pp 214–219.
3. Dieck, R. H., *I made that one up*, 1987.
4. Mace, C., *Essentials of Statistics for Scientists and Technologists*, pp 106–115, (Plenum Press, 1967).
5. *A sign in my office*, c. 1981.
6. Dieck, R. H., *One of my neat little rules*, c. 1975.
7. Bowker, A. H., and Lieberman, G. J., *Engineering Statistics*, second edition, pp 454–458 (Prentice Hall).
8. *Ibid.*, pp 452–454.
9. King, J. R., *Probability Charts for Decision Making*, pp 52–65, (Industrial Press, 1971).
10. Looney, S. W., and Gulledge, T. R., Jr., "Use of the Correlation Coefficient with Normal Probability Plots," *American Statistician*, vol. 39, no. 1, pp 75–79, Feb. 1985.

Exercises:

7-1. Outliers: Thompson's tau, τ, Problem

Consider data set:

1	−103	−121	−220
129	−38	25	−60
−56	89	8	−29
40	2	10	166
127	−35	334	−555

a. For given data without point -555, determine whether or not 334 is an outlier.
b. If it was, what is the next point to check? Is this point an outlier? If so, go to "c."
c. Are there any more outliers?

7-2. Curve Fitting Problem (see Table 7-3)
a. What is the curve fit with the lowest 2SEE for instruments CO_2 —A and B?
b. Are those lowest 2SEE's indicative of the best fits for the instruments and ranges noted?
c. What instruments and ranges have properly sized 2SEE's when the calibration gas errors are considered? Why?

7-3. Least Squares Curve Fit Problem:

Derive the equations needed for a least squares curve fit that is second order and forced through zero. (Hint: Use $Ax^2 + Bx + C = y$, where $C = 0$). Remember: Minimize (sum of squares of error term ϵ). $\epsilon = Ax^2 + Bx - y$.

7-4. Correlation Problems

Test Data Sets

A		B		C	
X	Y	X	Y	X	Y
0.8	0.5	1.7	-1.9	0.7	1.0
-0.7	-1.6	-7.8	-6.2	-2.0	3.2
4.8	4.3	-1.9	1.6	-1.5	0.8
2.6	2.4	2.8	1.5	2.2	-3.0
6.2	6.0	1.1	-0.9	1.8	-0.5
3.5	3.1	9.5	7.0	-0.3	0.2
-0.8	-0.9	1.4	2.7	-3.3	1.8
1.8	2.2	-2.6	-0.3	2.1	-1.4
-2.4	-2.3	2.5	-1.0	-1.2	-1.7
-0.2	0.4	-1.1	-1.9	3.4	-1.2
0.9	1.2	0.7	1.8	2.0	1.6
3.5	3.7	-0.8	1.7	-2.5	2.2

The correlation coefficients r_A, r_B, and r_C are $+0.986$, $+0.795$, and -0.628, respectively.
a. What are the 95% likely ranges for ρ_A, ρ_B, and ρ_C?
b. What are the 99% likely ranges for ρ_A, ρ_B, and ρ_C?
c. What r is significant? at 95%? at 99%?
d. Plot X vs. Y for each data set.
e. What is noticed about the plots? Recommend action.

f. *Compute a new* r_B. *Is it significant at 95%? at 99%?*
g. *What is learned?*

7-5. *Probability Plot Problem*

Data Sets: Error Data or Test Data			Median Ranks	
Set A	Set B	Set C	15 Points	12 Points
−0.25	0.10	3.60	0.045	0.056
−0.85	0.57	1.40	0.110	0.137
0.20	−0.42	−1.10	0.175	0.218
−0.65	0.76	2.90	0.240	0.298
−2.70	−1.80	4.20	0.305	0.379
−1.30	0.38	−2.80	0.370	0.460
0.85	1.08	3.20	0.435	0.540
−1.70	0.25	3.90	0.500	0.620
−0.50	−0.23	0.00	0.565	0.712
−0.05	−0.05	0.70	0.630	0.782
1.40		3.40	0.695	0.863
−2.10		2.10	0.760	0.944
−1.00			0.825	
0.45			0.890	
−1.50			0.955	

a. Assign median ranks to sets A and C. Remember to order the data from lowest to highest first (largest negative number is lowest). Calculate and assign median ranks to data set B.
b. Make up the probability plots for data sets A, B, and C. Remember to multiply the median ranks by 100 to get cumulative %.
c. What is observed for each:
   1) Line straight? Conclusion?
   2) $\overline{X}$?
   3) S_X?
   4) Outliers?
d. Calculate $\overline{X}$ and S_X for data sets A, B, and C. Compare with those in "c" above.
e. Any action recommended?

Unit 8:
Presentation of Results

UNIT 8

Presentation of Results

A frequently neglected part of any uncertainty analysis is the formulation of a compelling presentation of the content and impact of the results. The conclusion of an uncertainty analysis should yield information that a manager or experimentalist finds invaluable for the purposes of decision making. The primary purpose of doing an uncertainty analysis is to provide information that describes just how much faith can be placed in the results of a test. In this unit, the presentation of the results of a measurement uncertainty analysis will be detailed.

Learning Objectives — When you have completed this unit, you should:

A. Understand the need for a forceful, concise presentation of the results of an uncertainty analysis.

B. Be knowledgeable concerning the several presentation formats available.

C. Know how to assemble a compelling summary of uncertainty analysis results for management and customers.

8-1. General

The presentation of the results of an uncertainty analysis must be orderly, complete, and compelling. It must be orderly so that a novice (read that *manager*) can understand and apply the information. It must be complete so that the competency of the analyst is never called into question. Most who use the results of an uncertainty analysis don't understand its origin and just barely understand how to apply it. If there is an error or omission in the presentation, it will serve only to undermine the credibility of the analyst and the analysis. Credibility to an analytical person is all important. The presentation must be compelling so that its impact will be felt and its conclusions applied to the test results.

8-2. Presentation Content

The presentation of the uncertainty analysis results should include the following:

A. The total uncertainty, either U_{ADD} or U_{RSS}
- bias
- precision
- degrees of freedom
- error model chosen (from above two choices)

B. The elemental errors
- in measurement units
- in result units

C. Relative effect of error sources
- in percent of nominal level
- in percent of total uncertainty

D. Summary of the error propagation

8-3. Illustration

The simplest way to present a complicated uncertainty analysis is to illustrate it. Here, the illustration is for the uncertainty analysis of calculated turbine efficiency. It will be noted throughout that the detailed, boring, long, and gory equations that competent turbine performance analysts use for turbine efficiency are missing. Only five error sources are noted, although there are really dozens. Only the main drivers are presented here.

The uncertainty analysis presentation should start with the bottom line. Don't waste time and lose credibility by trying to give a manager too much detail at first. Work into it as needed for all to whom these results will be presented. One right way to present the turbine efficiency uncertainty bottom line is:

$$U_{ADD} = \pm 1.14\% \text{ at } 0.88 \text{ efficiency}$$

Note that the results are clearly percent of a level. The level is given for reference and the result is clearly associated with it. Do not get caught with presenting these results wrongly as:

$$U_{ADD} = \pm 1.14\% \text{ at } 88\% \text{ efficiency}$$

	Nominal Level	Bias ±(B)	Precision ±(2S)	Uncertainty* ±U
Efficiency Units	0.88	0.0056	0.0044	0.010
% of Nominal	100	0.64%	0.50%	1.14%

*Note that Uncertainty = U_{ADD} = ±[B + 2S]
Degrees of freedom >30

Table 8-1. Turbine Efficiency Bias and Precision Breakdown

The latter is an ambiguous report. Is the 1.14% of 88% or 1.003% in efficiency units, or is it 1.14% in efficiency units at a level of 88% efficiency? The former is clear; it is 1.14% at an efficiency of 0.88. Lesson number one is, therefore: *Be clearly unambiguous in your presentation* (please excuse the oversuperfluity in my redundance there).

Next, it is important to give some information concerning the 1.14% so that a competent technical person (usually not a manager) can better understand the impact of the uncertainty on the test results. Table 8-1 provides the next level of information.

In Table 8-1, the uncertainty model is clearly noted, as are the details of bias and precision along with nominal level and even the degrees of freedom. This level of competency in technical affairs (read that as "busy manager") is usually enough. However, the report should also include several more detailed tables of results.

Consider Table 8-2 in which the next level of detail is given. Note that throughout, $\nu = n - 1$, and N = 1 (that is, there is only one measurement of each parameter, but there may be many degrees of freedom for the S used and obtained from the

Error Source	Units	Nominal Level	Bias	Precision Index (S)	Degrees of Frdm.	Uncertainty* ±
Delta P	psid	4.68	0.0125	0.0025	>30	0.017
Air flow	lb/sec	147.	1.06	0.61	>30	2.28
Cooling air	lb/sec	27.	1.09	—	—	1.09
Fuel flow	lb/hr	15700.	44.1	40.5	>30	125.0
Burner P	psia	340.	1.0	0.5	>30	2.0
RSS (None needed)		—	—	—	—	—

*Note that Uncertainty = U_{ADD} = ±(B + 2S)

Table 8-2. Turbine Efficiency Elemental Errors in Measurement Units

s). Also, all $\nu > 30$ just for presentation simplicity. Additional columns may be added for n and/or N as appropriate, but they are not included here. In this unit, the emphasis is on the form of the presentation, not the technical detail.

In Table 8-2 the uncertainty model is again noted. Also, the errors cannot be root-sum-squared; they are of different units. The purpose for presenting this data is documentation of the error magnitudes and measurement levels that went into the uncertainty analysis. A table such as Table 8-2 should be followed by a table such as Table 8-3, in which the error sources are presented in "results" units; that is, in units of turbine efficiency for this example.

In Table 8-3, again the uncertainty model is noted. The RSS values are shown as are the final uncertainty, 0.0100, in turbine efficiency units, and the degrees of freedom. It is possible to RSS the errors here, because the error propagation into the same units, result units, has been done.

It is important to notice that the data in Table 8-3 show the uncertainty of each measurement in results units. However, the RSS of uncertainty is NOT DONE! The bias and precision are root-sum-squared only and then added to get the uncertainty.

Table 8-3 can be re-presented as Table 8-4 in which the errors in Table 8-3 are recomputed in terms of present of nominal turbine efficiency level.

It is important to notice that the data in Table 8-4, as the data in Table 8-3, show the uncertainty of each measurement in results units. However, the RSS of uncertainty is NOT DONE! The bias and precision are root-sum-squared only and then added to get the uncertainty.

Error Source	Bias	Precision Index (S)	Degrees of Frdm.	Uncertainty* ±
Delta P	0.0013	0.00025	>30	0.0018
Air flow	0.0030	0.00175	>30	0.0065
Cooling air	0.0039	—	—	0.0039
Fuel flow	0.0011	0.00075	>30	0.0026
Burner P	0.0021	0.00105	>30	0.0043
RSS	0.0056	0.00219	>30	0.0100

*Note that Uncertainty = U_{ADD} = ±(B + 2S)

Table 8-3. Turbine Efficiency Elemental Errors in Result Units

Error Source	Bias	Precision Index (S)	Degrees of Frdm.	Uncertainty* ±
Delta P	0.1477	0.0284	>30	0.2045
Air flow	0.3409	0.1989	>30	0.7386
Cooling air	0.4432	—	—	0.4432
Fuel flow	0.1250	0.0853	>30	0.2955
Burner P	0.2386	0.1193	>30	0.4772
RSS	0.6380	0.2487	>30	1.1354

*Note that Uncertainty = U_{ADD} = ±(B + 2S)

Table 8-4. Turbine Efficiency Elemental Errors in % of Nominal Level Units

Tables 8-3 and 8-4 are usually the most detailed tables of results a manager would need or like to see. However, there is another way to present the uncertainty results. The data in Table 8-3 can be reformatted to show directly the percent contribution to the total uncertainty by using Eqs. (8-1) and (8-2) below, in which the percent total uncertainty for each error term is computed.

$$B_i \text{ \% total uncertainty } = \{[(B_i)^2]/[(B_{RSS}) \times U_{ADD}]\} \times 100$$
$$(8-1)$$

$$2S_i \text{ \% total uncertainty } = \{[(2S_i)^2]/[(2S_{RSS}) \times U_{ADD}]\} \times 100$$
$$(8-2)$$

Eq. (8-2) assumes lots of degrees of freedom so that 2S can be used throughout. This is the only case in which these equations can be used properly; they cannot be used for tS.

Using Eqs. (8-1) and (8-2), Table 8-5, wherein the error sources are expressed in terms of their percent contribution to the total uncertainty, U_{ADD}, can be obtained.

Error Source	Bias	Precision Index (S)	Degrees of Frdm.	Uncertainty ±
Delta P	3.01	0.28	>30	—
Air flow	16.04	14.01	>30	—
Cooling air	27.12	—	—	—
Fuel flow	2.16	2.58	>30	—
Burner P	7.86	5.04	>30	—
RSS (not needed)	—	—	—	—

Table 8-5. Relative Effect of Error Sources in % of Total Uncertainty

There is no calculation of uncertainty and no calculation of final degrees of freedom in Table 8-5. However, the major error sources are seen clearly as air flow precision and cooling air bias. It is here that the major part of any uncertainty improvement program should be concentrated.

8-4. Summary

These tables, 8-1 through 8-5, provide the summary methods for presenting the results of an uncertainty analysis.

Appendix A:
Suggested Readings
and Study Materials

APPENDIX A

Suggested Readings and Study Materials

Independent Learning Modules:

One of your best sources of material for further reading and study of process control and instrumentation are the ILMs published by ISA. They are custom designed and created for this exact purpose. Place a *standing purchase order* to receive new ILMs as they are published. For a complete list of existing ILMs, refer to "ISA's Independent Learning Modules" in the front of this book.

Selected Titles:

Abernethy, Robert B., et al., *Handbook—Uncertainty in Gas Turbine Measurements*, (Arnold Engineering Development Center, Report Number AEDC-TR-73-5, Feb. 1973).

ANSI/ASME PTC 19.1-1985, *Instruments and Apparatus, Part 1, Measurement Uncertainty.*

Dixon, W. J., and Massey, Frank J., *Introduction to Statistical Analysis,* (McGraw-Hill, 1969).

King, James R., *Probability Charts for Decision Making,* (Industrial Press, 1971).

Ku, Harry H., *Notes on the Use of Error Propagation Formulas,* (National Bureau of Standards Report Number 9011, Dec. 1965).

Ku, Harry H., Editor, *Statistical Concepts and Procedures,* (National Bureau of Standards Special Publication 300, vol. 1, Feb. 1969).

Mack, C., *Essentials of Statistics for Scientists and Technologists,* (Plenum Press, 1967).

Practical Guide Series

This is a new ISA Series with seventeen planned volumes. The emphasis is on the practice of process measurement and control.

Appendix B:
Glossary of Measurement Uncertainty Terminology

APPENDIX B

Glossary of Measurement Uncertainty Terminology

addition uncertainty model—The uncertainty model where the bias and precision error components are linearly added together. $U = \pm (B + t_{95}S)$

back-to-back tests—Tests run so closely in time that there is no time for instrument drift or calibrations. These tests have zero bias error.

bad data—Data that disproves "my" theory or thesis.

Benard's formula—The formula used to compute median ranks.

bias—Systematic error that does not change for the duration of an experiment or test.

bias limit—The estimate of the true bias error.

blunders—Major engineering errors.

calibration errors—Errors resulting from measurement system calibration.

categorize errors—What can be done to ease error analysis bookkeeping.

concomitant functions—Several methods for making the same measurement or calculation that are independent.

confidence—A statistical expression of percent likelihood.

correlation—The relationship between two data sets. It is not necessarily an evidence of cause and effect.

correlation coefficients—The statistic used to calculate correlation.

coverage—A nonstatistic intended to express the likelihood that the true value lies within some interval about the biased average.

curve fitting—A least-squares method for estimating a curve shape from a data set of X and Y paired values.

curve fitting cautions—The risks of least-square curve fitting

data acquisition errors—A category of error sources related to the method of data acquisition.

data reduction errors—A category of error sources associated with the data reduction process.

delta—The difference between two values.

degrees of freedom—The amount of room left for error.

dithering—The numerical method for evaluating influence coefficients or sensitivity coefficients.

doubter—Personality: "I don't believe in all that uncertainty mumbo-jumbo."

error—(Error) = (measured) − (true). It is the difference between the measured value and the true value.

Gaussian-normal distribution—The standard expression of the frequency distribution for the most common error data.

good data—Data that proves "my" thesis. Data "I" expected.

group errors—Errors grouped into categories of calibration, data acquisition, data reduction, or errors of method.

Grubb's technique—An outlier identifying technique that identifies few potential outliers.

histogram—Frequency bar chart of a sample of data with the data values the abscissa and the frequency of occurrence the ordinate.

indifferent—Personality: "This is not my favorite subject."

influence coefficient—An expression of the influence an error source has on a test result. It is the ratio of the change in the result for an incremental change in an input variable or parameter measured.

interlaboratory—Comparisons made on the same specimen or artifact in order to evaluate the existence and magnitude of bias error.

least count—The minimum difference between measurements when plotted on probability paper. The smallest increment for a measurement system.

manager—Get the story to him or her in the first two sentences and make it simple.

matrix analysis—A simple procedure for separating real variation in time and space from precision error. The remaining variation is called sampling error.

measurement uncertainty—The maximum possible error that may reasonably occur. Errors larger than the measurement uncertainty should rarely occur.

median ranks—Using Benard's formula, the percentile rank each data point should occupy if the data sample is normally distributed.

nonsymmetrical bias limit—The bias limit for which there is an uneven likelihood that the true bias error, β, lies on one side of the biased average or the other.

nonsymmetrical uncertainty—The uncertainty limit for which there is an uneven likelihood that the true value lies on one side of the biased average or the other.

normality—The state of a data set when it is equivalent to a Gaussian-normal distribution.

ostrich—Personality: "I don't want you guys putting fuzz bands on my data."

outliers—"Wild" data; data outside the normally expected data scatter.

outlier rejection—An objective procedure for eliminating outlier data, usually Thompson's τ.

pooling—The combination by squares of several standard deviations, each obtained from a sample from the same population. The pooled standard deviation is a better estimate of the population standard deviation than any one sample.

precision—The name given random error sources.

precision error—The same as random error.

precision error sources—Error sources that contribute scatter to the test result data set.

precision index—The standard deviation of the error data divided by the square root of the number of data points to be averaged: $S_{ij} = s_{ij}/\sqrt{N_{ij}}$

presentation—The method for providing the results of an uncertainty analysis in compelling fashion.

pride—The human factor most to blame for estimating bias limits too low.

probability plots—A graphical technique for assessing the normality of a data set. Data that plots as a straight line on probability paper is normally distributed.

propagation of error—The analytical technique for evaluating the impact of an error source on the test result. It employs the use of influence (or sensitivity) coefficients.

random error—The same as precision error. This is error that causes scatter in the test result.

root-sum-square uncertainty mode—The uncertainty mode where the bias and precision error components are summed in quadrature. $U = \pm[(B)^2 + (t_{95}S)^2]^{1/2}$

sampling error—A precision error source related to the distribution of data in a sample taken from a group of locations such as inside a pipe.

sensitivity—Same as influence coefficient.

standard deviation—Standard deviation of a data sample is s:
$s = [\Sigma(X_i - \overline{X})^2/(N - 1)]^{1/2}$

standard error of the mean—The standard deviation of a data sample divided by the number of data points averaged.

Student's t—The t statistic.

systematic error—The bias error. The error sources that are constant for the duration of the experiment.

symmetrical bias error—The bias error type with equal probability of the true bias error, β, being on either side of the biased average.

Taylor's series error propagation—An error propagation method for determining the impact of an error source on the test result.

Thompson's τ technique—An outlier rejection technique that sometimes identifies nonoutlier data as potential outliers.

true value—The desired result of an experimental measurement.

Welch-Satterthwaite—The approximation method for determining the number of degrees of freedom in the precision index of the result.

weighted bias—The bias limit associated with the weighted average.

weighted precision—The precision error associated with the weighted average.

weighted degrees of freedom—The degrees of freedom associated with the weighted average.

weighted uncertainty—The uncertainty limit associated with the weighted average.

weighting—The method of weighting a group of averages of the same test result by the uncertainties of their independent measurement techniques.

uncertainty limit—The interval about the biased average into which the true value is expected to lie with some stated coverage.

units of error—The expression of the engineering or scientific units for an error analysis. Error units must be the same in order to root-sum-square bias limits or precision indexes.

Appendix C:
Nomenclature

APPENDIX C

Nomenclature

A_t = The average of all measurements at time t across all locations l when performing an analysis of sampling error.

a = The first-order constant (slope) in a typical straight line of the formula $Y = aX + b$.

B = The symmetrical systematic error component of the uncertainty. It is the symmetrical bias limit of the result.

$\underline{B}$ = The weighted symmetrical systematic error component of the weighted uncertainty.

$B = \pm[\Sigma\Sigma(b_{ij})^2]^{1/2}$ where B and b_{ij} have the same units.

$B = \pm\{\Sigma\Sigma[(\partial F/\partial V_{ij})^2(b_{ij})^2]\}^{1/2}$ where B is in result units and where the result is obtained with a function $F(V_{11}, V_{21}, \ldots V_{12}, V_{22}, \ldots V_{ninj})$ with i_i times j variables, V_{ij}, each with its own b_{ij} in its own units.

B^+ = The positive component of a nonsymmetrical systematic error component of the uncertainty.

$B^+ = -[\Sigma\Sigma(b_{ij}^+)^2]^{1/2}$ where B^+ and b_{ij}^+ have the same units.

$B^+ = -\{\Sigma\Sigma[(\partial F/\partial V_{ij})^2(b_{ij}^+)^2]\}^{1/2}$ where B^+ is in result units and where the result is obtained with a function $F(V_{11}, V_{21}, \ldots V_{12}, V_{22}, \ldots V_{ninj})$ with i_i times j variables, V_{ij}, each with its own b_{ij} in its own units.

B^- = The negative component of a nonsymmetrical systematic error component of the uncertainty.

$B^- = +[\Sigma\Sigma(b_{ij}^-)^2]^{1/2}$ where B^- and b_{ij}^- have the same units.

$B^- = +\{\Sigma\Sigma[(\partial F/\partial V_{ij})^2(b_{ij}^-)^2]\}^{1/2}$ where B^- is in result units and where the result is obtained with a function $F(V_{11}, V_{21}, \ldots V_{12}, V_{22}, \ldots V_{ninj})$ with i times j variables, V_{ij}, each with its own b_{ij} in its own units.

b = The zero-order constant (intercept) in a typical straight line of the formula $Y = aX + b$.

b = A symmetrical elemental bias limit. b is usually subscripted; see b_{ij}.

b_{ij} = The symmetrical bias limit estimate for error source i in error category j.

b^+ = The positive component of a nonsymmetrical elemental bias limit. b^+ is usually subscripted; see b_{ij}^+.

b_{ij}^+ = The positive component of a nonsymmetrical bias limit for error source i in error category j.

b^- = The negative component of a nonsymmetrical elemental bias limit. b^- is usually subscripted; see b_{ij}^-.

b_{ij}^- = The negative component of a nonsymmetrical bias limit for error source i in error category j.

d.f. = The degrees of freedom associated with a standard deviation or precision index. d.f. is often subscripted.

D_{lt} = The measurement at location l and time t, used in a "matrix" analysis of sampling error.

e = The generic descriptor for error, e could be either bias or precision; e is often subscripted.

e = The base of the natural log where appropriate.

F = Fahrenheit degrees, usually written as °F.

F = A function of some variables, usually written F(V)

i = The number of the error source in a category, j.

j = The number of the error category. Usually there are four: calibration, data acquisition, data reduction, and errors of method.

k = A subscript counter.

K = The number of constants determined in a least-squares curve fit.

l = The location of a measurement when performing an analysis of sampling error.

M = The number of times a measurement is averaged.

$\mathfrak{M}$ = The number of times an experiment or test is repeated and the result averaged.

m = The number of redundant measurements of n repeats that may be pooled.

N = The number of data points or measurements averaged to obtain a measurement of one parameter such as temperature. N is often subscripted.

N_{ij} = The number of data points or measurements averaged to obtain the average value for category i and error source j. (See S_{ij}.)

n = The number of data points used to calculate a standard deviation, S_X or s_{ij}. n is often subscripted.

n = The number of locations, l, when performing an analysis of sampling error.

n_{ij} = The number of data points used to calculate s_{ij}.

P = The symbol for pressure. P is sometimes subscripted.

$P_{0.50}$ = The 50 percentile median rank. It is obtained with Benard's formula: $P_{0.50} = (i - 0.3)/(N + 0.4)$, where i is the ith data point after ordering from lowest to highest value and N is the number of data points in the data set.

psi = Pounds per square inch.

R = A generic result when more than one variable or parameter are combined to yield the result.

r = The correlation coefficient of a data set or sample.

S = The precision index of the result.

$\underline{\underline{S}}$ = The weighted precision index of the result.

$S = \pm[\Sigma\Sigma(S_{ij})^2]^{1/2}$, where S and S_{ij} have the same units.

$S = \pm\{\Sigma\Sigma[(\partial F/\partial V_{ij})^2(S_{ij})^2]\}^{1/2}$, where S is in result units and where the result is obtained with a function $F(V_{11}, V_{21}, \ldots V_{12}, V_{22}, \ldots V_{ni}, V_{nj})$ with i times j variables, V_{ij}, each with its own S_{ij} in its own units. ·

S_{CAL} = The standard deviation of the calibration data.

SEE = The standard error of estimate. This describes the data scatter around a fitted line. It is analogous to S_X or s_{ij}, which describes the data scatter around an average.
$SEE = \pm\{[\Sigma(Y_i - Y_{ci})^2/(n - K)]^{1/2}\}$

s_{ij} = The standard deviation of error source i in error category j.

$s_{ij} = \pm\{[\Sigma(X_{ijk} - \overline{X}_{ij})^2/(n_{ij} - 1)]^{1/2}\}$. (Note: the sum is over k.)

S_i = The precision index for the errors in category i. (Note: sum was done over j error sources.)

S_{ij} = The precision index for error source i in error category j:
$$S_{ij} = \pm[s_{ij}/(N_{ij})^{1/2}]$$

S_{IL} = The standard deviation of the interlaboratory data.

S_X = The standard deviation of a data set:
$$S_X = \pm\{[\Sigma(X_i - \overline{X})^2/(n - 1)]^{1/2}\}$$

$S_{\overline{X}}$ = The estimate of the standard deviation of the average for a data set of N values.

$$S_{\overline{X}} = \pm[S_x/(N)^{1/2}]$$

S_{pooled} = The pooled standard deviation obtained from several estimates of the same population standard deviation.

$S_{X, pooled} = S_{pooled}$

S_Δ = The standard deviation of the difference between pairs of redundant measurements.

T = The symbol for temperature. T is sometimes subscripted.

TC = Thermocouple.

t = The time of a measurement when performing an analysis of sampling error.

$t_{\alpha, \nu}$ = The t-statistic. The uncertainty uses only 95% confidence, t_{95}, for the appropriate degrees of freedom, ν. The usual notation is just t_{95}.

$t_{95}S$ = The random error component of the uncertainty. It is the precision error of the result.

$t_{95}s_{ij}$ = An estimate of the precision error for error source i in error category j.

U = The result uncertainty.

$\underline{U}$ = The weighted result uncertainty.

U^+ = The positive component of a nonsymmetrical uncertainty interval.

U^- = The negative component of a nonsymmetrical uncertainty interval.

U_{ADD} = The additive model uncertainty. This has $\approx 99\%$ coverage.
$$U_{ADD} = \pm(B + t_{95}S)$$

U_{ADD}^+ = The positive component of the nonsymmetrical uncertainty interval for the additive model uncertainty. This is used for $\approx 99\%$ coverage.
$$U_{ADD}^+ = -(B^+ + t_{95}S)$$

U_{ADD}^- = The negative component of the nonsymmetrical uncertainty interval for the additive model uncertainty. This is used for $\approx 99\%$ coverage.
$$U_{ADD}^- = +|B^- - t_{95}S|$$

U_{RSS} = The root-sum-square model uncertainty. This has $\approx 95\%$ coverage.
$$U_{RSS} = \pm[(B)^2 + (t_{95}S)^2]^{1/2}$$

U_{RSS}^+ = The positive component of the nonsymmetrical uncertainty interval for the root-sum-square model uncertainty. This is used for $\approx 95\%$ coverage.
$$U_{RSS}^+ = -[(B^+)^2 + (t_{95}S)^2]^{1/2}$$

U_{RSS}^- = The negative component of the nonsymmetrical uncertainty interval for the root-sum-square model uncertainty. This is used for $\approx 95\%$ coverage.
$$U_{RSS}^- = +[(B^-)^2 + (t_{95}S)^2]^{1/2}$$

$$U_{99} = U_{ADD} = \pm(B + t_{95}S)$$
$$U_{99}^+ = U_{ADD}^+ = -(B^+ + t_{95}S)$$
$$U_{99}^- = U_{ADD}^- = +|B^- - t_{95}S|$$
$$U_{95} = U_{RSS} = \pm[(B)^2 + (t_{95}S)^2]^{1/2}$$
$$U_{95}^+ = U_{RSS}^+ = -[(B^+)^2 + (t_{95}S)^2]^{1/2}$$
$$U_{95}^- = U_{RSS}^- = +[(B^-)^2 + (t_{95}S)^2]^{1/2}$$

V = A generic variable or parameter being measured. V is often subscripted.

W_i = The weight assigned the ith average in computing a weighted average. W_i is also the weight assigned to each precision, bias, and uncertainty when computing the weighted precision, bias, and uncertainty.

X = The generic data point or measurement, a population value. X is often subscripted.

X = The abscissa value of a data point (X, Y). X is often subscripted.

$\overline{X}$ = The average of a data set of X_i data points or measurements.

$\overline{X}_i$ = The ith $\overline{X}$.

Y = The ordinate value of a data point (X, Y). Y is often subscripted.

Y_{ci} = The Y value of a fitted curve at the point X_i.

α = The symbol for the percent coverage for the Student's t distribution, usually taken as 0.95 for 95%.

β = The true bias error for a particular measurement.

γ = The ratio of specific heats for a gas.

∂ = The symbol indicating partial differentiation.

$\delta = \beta + \epsilon$ = the true total error for a particular measurement.

δ_{lt} = The difference between the measurement at each location, l, and its time, t, average, A_t, when performing an analysis of sampling error.

$\overline{\delta}_l$ = The average of all δ_{lt} at location, l, across time, t, when performing an analysis of sampling error.

Δ = The difference between two measurements. Δ is often subscripted.

$\overline{\Delta}$ = The average of a group of differences between two measurements.

$\overline{\Delta}$ = The average of the Δ_{lt} values when performing an analysis of sampling error.

Δ_{lt} = The values of the residual errors after the linear variation in time and space are averaged out when performing an analysis of sampling error.

ϵ = The true random error of a measurement.

ϵ_i = The difference between a data point Y_i value and a fitted line at the point X_i; $\epsilon_i = (Y_i - Y_{ci}) = [Y_i - (aX_i + b)]$

η_c = The symbol for compressor efficiency.

Θ_{ij} = The influence (or sensitivity) coefficient of the result. It is the effect on the result of error source i (bias or precision) in error category j.

$\Theta_{ij} = (\partial F / \partial V_{ij})$

μ = The true average for an entire population.

ν = d.f. = degrees of freedom for a standard deviation or a precision index or SEE. ν is often subscripted. For s_{ij}; S_{ij}, S_X, or $S_{\overline{X}}$; d.f. = n

− 1 where n is the number of data points used to calculate s_{ij}; S_{ij}, S_X, or $S_{\bar{X}}$ for SEE, $\nu = n - K$ where n is the number of data points in a curve fit and K is the number of constants calculated for the fit.

$\underline{\underline{\nu}} = \underline{\underline{\text{d.f.}}}$ = weighted degrees of freedom.

$\pi = 3.14159$

$\rho = $ The true population correlation coefficient.

$\sigma = $ The standard deviation of an entire population of data (or measurements), sometimes called σ_X.

$\sigma_{\bar{X}} = $ The standard deviation of the average of a population.

$\tau = $ Thompson's Tau. This is used to identify outliers with the Thompson's Tau technique.

Appendix D:
Student's t for 95% Confidence

APPENDIX D

Student's t for 95% Confidence

ν	t_{95}	ν	t_{95}
1	12.706	16	2.120
2	4.303	17	2.110
3	3.182	18	2.101
4	2.776	19	2.093
5	2.571	20	2.086
6	2.447	21	2.080
7	2.365	22	2.074
8	2.306	23	2.069
9	2.262	24	2.064
10	2.228	25	2.060
11	2.201	26	2.056
12	2.179	27	2.052
13	2.160	28	2.048
14	2.145	29	2.045
15	2.131	∞*	2.000*

For uncertainty analysis, for $\nu \geq 30$, t = 2.000.

Appendix E:
5% Significant Thompson's τ

APPENDIX E

5% Significant Thompson's τ

(Odds against rejecting a good data point are 20 to 1 or less)

Sample Size	τ	Sample Size	τ	Sample Size	τ
3	1.150	16	1.865	29	1.910
4	1.393	17	1.871	30	1.911
5	1.572	18	1.876	31	1.913
6	1.656	19	1.881	32	1.914
7	1.711	20	1.885	33	1.916
8	1.749	21	1.889	34	1.917
9	1.777	22	1.893	35	1.919
10	1.798	23	1.896	36	1.920
11	1.815	24	1.899	37	1.921
12	1.829	25	1.902	38	1.922
13	1.840	26	1.904	39	1.923
14	1.849	27	1.906	40	1.924
15	1.858	28	1.908		

Appendix F:
Areas Under the Normal Curve

APPENDIX F

Areas Under the Normal Curve

Number of σ	Fraction of Area	Number of σ	Fraction of Area
−3.0	0.0014	0.0	0.5000
−2.5	0.0062	0.1	0.5398
−2.3	0.0107	0.2	0.5793
−2.0	0.0228	0.3	0.6179
−1.9	0.0287	0.4	0.6554
−1.8	0.0359	0.5	0.3085
−1.7	0.0446	0.6	0.7257
−1.6	0.0548	0.7	0.7580
−1.5	0.0668	0.8	0.7881
−1.4	0.0808	0.9	0.8159
−1.3	0.0968	1.0	0.8413
−1.2	0.1151	1.1	0.8643
−1.1	0.1357	1.2	0.8849
−1.0	0.1587	1.3	0.9032
−0.9	0.1841	1.4	0.9192
−0.8	0.2119	1.5	0.9332
−0.7	0.2420	1.6	0.9452
−0.6	0.2743	1.7	0.9554
−0.5	0.3085	1.8	0.9641
−0.4	0.3446	1.9	0.9713
−0.3	0.3821	2.0	0.9772
−0.2	0.4207	2.3	0.9893
−0.1	0.4602	2.5	0.9938
		3.0	0.9986

Note that "Number of σ" is the number of standard deviations equivalent to the cumulative area under the normal curve. It is to be used in probability plotting as the linear horizontal axis when probability plotting paper is not available.

Note that "Fraction of Area" is the cumulative area under the curve for the number of σ shown. When probability plotting, the median rank (not multiplied by 100) is equivalent to the "Fraction of Area." Interpolation between the data given is done linearly.

Appendix G:
Pressure Instrumentation
Selection Example

APPENDIX G

Pressure Instrumentation Selection Example

This is a detailed instrumentation selection example in which pressure instrumentation is selected for a fictional flight test of an aircraft inlet. The pressure instrumentation selected needs to measure dynamic and steady-state pressures in the engine inlet of the aircraft. It is a problem that is closely analogous to measuring pressure profiles and averages in a pipe or duct.

This instrument selection example has six major parts:

1. Define the test setup.

2. Estimate the elemental errors for each pressure transducer type.

3. Root-sum-square bias and precision errors for each transducer type.

4. Root-sum-square bias and precision errors from each transducer for each test condition.

5. Add bias and precision to obtain U_{ADD}.

6. Repeat analysis to test the effect of proposed improvements.

1. Define the test setup.

For this test, ram recovery (total pressure) will be measured with three calibrated or reference absolute pressure transducers and 39 delta pressure transducers, which, when referenced to the three reference transducers, will provide a measurement of the steady-state pressure profile in the engine inlet duct (or in a test pipe). However, for this analysis, it is also necessary to measure inlet distortion. This is done by using the 39 delta pressure transducers to establish the pressure level at each position in the inlet and then measure pressure fluctuation with high-response transducers at each position.

For this test sequence, two test conditions are of interest. They are summarized as follows. Each typical pressure level or response is noted.

Low altitude, supersonic

$$P_T = 36 \text{ psia}; \ \Delta P = 4.4 \text{ psid}; \ P_{HR} = 0.8 \text{ psi}$$

High altitude, subsonic

$$P_T = 2 \text{ psia}; \ \Delta P = 0.38 \text{ psid}; \ P_{HR} = 0.3 \text{ psi}$$

In the above, P_T = total pressure or ram pressure
ΔP = the typical delta pressure at one of the 39 locations
P_{HR} = high-response pressure

As a part of the test setup definition, it is necessary to consider carefully the definition of transducer nonlinearity, end-point fit, hysteresis, and other terms. These are illustrated in Fig. D-1.

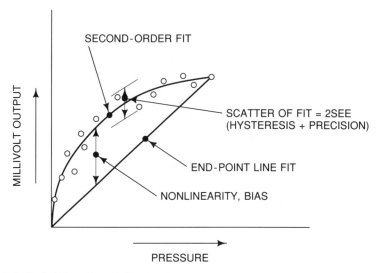

Fig. D-1. Typical Transducer Calibration Curve

Fig. D-1 illustrates several terms associated with the use of transducer calibration data. These terms are the scatter of the fit, hysteresis, precision, nonlinearity, end-point line, and second-order fit.

The scatter of the fit is illustrative of the variation in data about a least-squares second-order curve fit for a typical transducer. This scatter is due to two physical effects: hysteresis and precision error. The hysteresis is the difference in transducer response experienced when calibration data taken with monotonically increasing pressures is compared with that taken with monotonically decreasing pressures. The precision error effect is seen to cause scatter in the data no matter how the calibration data is taken.

The nonlinearity is a measure of the difference of the true transducer response curve with that of a straight line fit through the end points of the data, that is, from zero to the maximum data point taken. It is usually the maximum difference possible between the data second-order fit and the end-point straight line.

In this test example, it is necessary to redefine the nonlinearity. Consider Fig. D-2, in which a second definition of nonlinearity is presented. The "most common" definition remains presented as it was in Fig. D-1, and the second definition for "this test" has been shown as well. This definition is the difference between the transducer response curve (second-order fit) and the end-point line but at the pressure region of interest. In this test, it is necessary to have high-range transducers to assure they will not be damaged by pressure spikes. Most of the data needed, however, is to be taken at the low end of the transducer performance. Hence, it is necessary to express nonlinearity in the region of interest, not by the usual definition. This is another important lesson in data analysis and uncertainty analysis: *Fit the analysis method to the physics of the test problem; don't try to force the data or methods into a mold.* The physics of the process are all important.

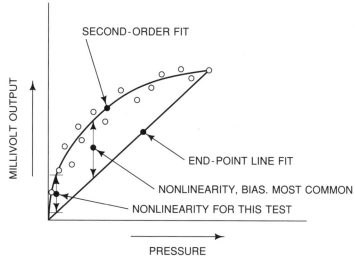

Fig. D-2. Low End Nonlinearity Evaluation

It is important to note that in the test setup the ranges of the transducers need to be specified. To start with, these ranges are as follows:

Reference standard transducers (3) = 0–50 psia

Delta pressure transducers (39) = 0–15 psid

High-response transducers (39) = 0–50 psi

2. Estimate the elemental errors for each pressure transducer type.

Now comes the most important and often the most difficult part of any uncertainty analysis. The elemental errors need to be estimated for each transducer type. Most of these errors will be obtained from calibration data. Only where necessary will error estimates be taken from manufacturer's specifications.

(Manufacturer's specifications are often a most misleading source of uncertainty information and should be avoided if at all possible. This author once heard an experimentalist say that when using manufacturer's specifications for errors he takes what the literature says and doubles the errors quoted. He takes what the salesman says and multiplies by ten! Sounds like good advice [tongue in cheek].)

(Note that in all the following tables, many degrees of freedom are assumed so that 2S may be used for tS throughout.)

For the 0–50 psia transducer, typical elemental errors are shown in Table D-1. Note that in Table D-1 (and those following) the test conditions are approximated; that is, the nonlinearity is at the approximate test pressure of interest, the zero shift is representative of the transducer in question, and the sensitivity

Error Source	Bias (psi)	Precision (2S, psi)
A) Calibration	±0.005	N/A
B) Nonlinearity (@ 36 psia)	0 to +0.036	±0.037
C) Hysteresis/Precision	N/A	±0.0434
D) Zero Shift	±0.080	N/A
(0.01% F.S. / °F @ +16°F)		
E) Sensitivity Shift		
(0.01%R / °F @ +16°F)		
E1) Low Alt., Supersonic	N/A	±0.058
E2) High Alt., Subsonic	N/A	±0.032
F) RSS Low Alt., Supersonic	±0.088	$\pm 0.081/\sqrt{3} = \pm 0.047$
G) RSS High Alt., Subsonic	±0.088	$\pm 0.057/\sqrt{3} = \pm 0.033$

Table D-1. 0–50 psia Reference Standard Transducer Elemental Errors

shift represents the transducer response typical of the temperature change expected in the experiment. Note also that the precision terms are divided by the square root of the number of sensors averaged, three in Table D-1 and as appropriate in the tables following.

For the 0–15 psid delta pressure transducer, the elemental errors are as shown in Table D-2. Note that in Table D-2 there are some nonsymmetrical bias errors. They are not shown to affect the RSS values because they are so small. If they did, the RSS values would have also been nonsymmetrical. Note also that the precision terms are divided by the square root of the number of sensors averaged, 39 in this case.

Now note the elemental errors in the 0–50 psi high-response transducers shown in Table D-3. Note here that there is no bias term in the elemental errors of a high-response transducer. That is because all the experimenter is interested in is the variation around some mean. Here, the mean is defined as the value of the delta pressure transducer as compared to the reference standard average. Note also that the precision terms are not divided by the square root of the number of sensors, 39, because there is no averaging. When measuring the dynamic pressure disturbances in a duct, each reading is important and averages have little meaning.

Error Source	Bias (psi)	Precision (2S, psi)
A) Calibration	±0.0015	N/A
B) Nonlinearity		
B1) Low Alt., Supersonic	0 to +0.0078	±0.036
B2) High Alt., Subsonic	0 to −0.009	±0.040
C) Hysteresis/Precision	N/A	±0.0133
D) Zero Shift	±0.024	N/A
(0.01% F.S. / °F @ +16°F)		
E) Sensitivity Shift		
(0.01%R / °F @ +16°F)		
E1) Low Alt., Supersonic	N/A	±0.0070
E2) High Alt., Subsonic	N/A	±0.0006
F) RSS Low Alt., Supersonic	±0.025	$\pm 0.039/\sqrt{39} = \pm 0.0062$
G) RSS High Alt., Subsonic	±0.027	$\pm 0.042/\sqrt{39} = \pm 0.0066$

Table D-2. 0–15 psid Delta Pressure Transducer Elemental Errors

Error Source	Bias (psi)	Precision (2S, psi)
A) Calibration	N/A	N/A
B) Nonlinearity	N/A	N/A
C) Hysteresis/Precision	N/A	±0.045
D) Zero Shift	N/A	N/A
E) Sensitivity Shift (±2.2%R @ −65 to +450°F)		
E1) Low Alt., Supersonic	N/A	±0.0176
E2) High Alt., Subsonic	N/A	±0.0066
F) RSS Low Alt., Supersonic	N/A	±0.048
G) RSS High Alt., Subsonic	N/A	±0.046

Table D-3. 0–50 psi High-Response Transducer Elemental Errors

3. Root-sum-square bias and precision errors for each transducer type.

Note that in the three tables, D-1, D-2, and D-3, the RSS of bias and precision has been completed for each transducer type (lines F and G in the tables). Note also that lines F) and G) represent 2S (that's capital S). It represents twice the precision index for each transducer type in Tables D-1, D-2, and D-3. In the uncertainty analysis summary following, it is the value that is RSS'd to get the precision error. Next is obtaining the RSS value for each bias and precision error from each transducer type for the test condition in question.

4. Root-sum-square bias and precision errors from each transducer for each test condition.

5. Add bias and precision to obtain U_{ADD}.

Here the data is summarized in Table D-4 for the total pressure or ram recovery uncertainty. For this uncertainty, it is necessary to recognize that the total pressure (or ram recovery) involves the addition of the average readings from the reference transducers and the average readings from the delta pressure transducers.

Test Condition	Bias (psi)	Precision (2S, psi)	Table Line Reference
A) Low Alt., Supersonic			
A1) Reference @ 36 psia	±0.088	±0.047	D-1:Line F)
A2) Delta P. @ 4.4 psid	±0.025	±0.0062	D-2:Line F)
A3) RSS @ 40.4 psia	±0.091	±0.047	
A4) U_{ADD} = ±(0.091 + 0.047) = ±0.138 psi, or, ±0.343%R @ 40.4 psia			
B) High Alt., Subsonic			
B1) Reference @ 2 psia	±0.088	±0.033	D-1:Line G)
B2) Delta P. @ 0.38 psid	±0.027	±0.0066	D-2:Line G)
B3) RSS @ 2.38 psia	±0.092	±0.0337	
B4) U_{ADD} = ±(0.092 + 0.0337) = ±0.126 psi, or, ±5.3%R @ 2.38 psia			

Table D-4. Total Pressure (or Ram Recovery) Uncertainty

Test Condition	Bias (psi)	Precision (2S, psi)	Table Line Reference
A) Low Alt., Supersonic			
A1) Delta P @ 4.4 psid	±0.025	±0.039	D-2:Line F)
A2) High Response @ 0.8 psi	N/A	±0.048	D-3:Line F)
A3) RSS @ 5.2 psia	±0.025	±0.062	
A4) $U_{ADD} = \pm(0.025 + 0.062) = \pm0.087$ psi, or, $\pm1.67\%R$ @ 5.2 psia			
B) High Alt., Subsonic			
B1) Delta P @ 0.38 psia	±0.027	±0.042	D-2:Line G)
B2) High Response @ 0.3 psi	N/A	±0.046	D-3:Line G)
B3) RSS @ 0.68 psia	±0.027	±0.062	
B4) $U_{ADD} = \pm(0.027 + 0.062) = \pm0.087$ psi, or, $\pm13.1\%R$ @ 0.68 psia			

Table D-5. Dynamic Distortion Pressure Uncertainty

In Table D-4, the U_{ADD}'s (lines A4 and B4) represent the uncertainty of total pressure measurement (or ram recovery) at low altitude, supersonic and high altitude, subsonic conditions, respectively.

Table D-5 summarizes the uncertainty analysis for dynamic distortion pressure. Here, it is necessary to recognize the test setup results in adding the pressure measurements of both the delta pressure transducers and the high-response transducers at each location. No averaging is done.

In Table D-5, the U_{ADD}'s (lines A4 and B4) represent the uncertainty of dynamic pressure measurement at low altitude, supersonic and high altitude, subsonic conditions, respectively.

6. Repeat analysis to test effect of proposed improvements.

If the uncertainties computed up to now are too large, the uncertainty analysis itself can be used to determine what actions, if taken, would yield improved uncertainty.

First, a shift to a lower range delta pressure transducer will be evaluated. Then a second-order curve fit will be examined instead of the end-point straight line used in the foregoing analysis. After that, an improved temperature correction for the high-response transducers will be covered.

First, the shift to a lower range delta pressure transducer is examined. Here, the uncertainty of a 0–5 psid delta pressure transducer will be compared to that of a 0–15 psid delta pressure transducer. Consider the error data in Table D-6, and note that the calibration error is the same as for the 0–15 psid transducer documented in Table D-2. This is because they have the same calibration source and methods. However, every other error source is reduced substantially. The resulting RSS errors on lines F) and G) in Table D-6 illustrate in an objective way what most experimenters already believe subjectively to be true; that is, lower range instruments should be used for lower level measurements.

The data in Table D-6 can be summarized in a fashion similar to the data in Table D-2 to yield an uncertainty in both the total (ram) pressure and dynamic

Error Source	Bias (psi)	Precision (2S, psi)
A) Calibration	± 0.0015	N/A
B) Nonlinearity		
B1) Low Alt., Supersonic	0 to +0.0026	± 0.012
B2) High Alt., Subsonic	0 to −0.003	± 0.013
C) Hysteresis/Precision	N/A	± 0.0044
D) Zero Shift	± 0.008	N/A
(0.01% F.S. / °F @ +16°F)		
E) Sensitivity Shift		
(0.01%R / °F @ +16°F)		
E1) Low Alt., Supersonic	N/A	± 0.0070
E2) High Alt., Subsonic	N/A	± 0.0006
F) RSS Low Alt., Supersonic	± 0.008	± 0.0146 / $\sqrt{39}$ = ± 0.0023
G) RSS High Alt., Subsonic	± 0.008	± 0.0137 / $\sqrt{39}$ = ± 0.0022

Table D-6. 0–5 psid Delta Pressure Transducer Elemental Errors

pressure readings for the duct. However, the details of that will be left to be reviewed by the student. The resulting impact on the total (ram) and dynamic pressure uncertainties will be summarized later in Table D-9.

Another method for reducing error in these delta pressure transducers is to use second-order curve fits instead of the end-point straight lines. The impact of this change on the 0–15 psid transducers is shown in Table D-7.

Note that the impact of using the curve fits is to reduce the nonlinearity terms to zero. Note also that, although this is a good idea, it has a negligible impact on the final RSS error summaries.

The next thing that can be tried is to improve on the uncertainty of the high-response transducers by improving their temperature conditioning. This will reduce the impact of the sensitivity shift with temperature. The impact of this change is shown in Table D-8. Here, too, although the change in temperature control is significant, as shown by comparing precisions of the low altitudes (lines E1) and E2) in Tables D-3) with those in Table D-8, the effect on the uncertainty will be negligible.

Error Source	Bias (psi)	Precision (2S, psi)
A) Calibration	± 0.0015	N/A
B) Nonlinearity		
B1) Low Alt., Supersonic	0.0	± 0.036
B2) High Alt., Subsonic	0.0	± 0.040
C) Hysteresis/Precision	N/A	± 0.0133
D) Zero shift	± 0.024	N/A
(0.01% F.S. / °F @ + 16°F)		
E) Sensitivity Shift		
(0.01%R / °F @ +16°F)		
E1) Low Alt., Supersonic	N/A	± 0.0070
E2) High Alt., Subsonic	N/A	± 0.0006
F) RSS Low Alt., Supersonic	± 0.024	± 0.039 / $\sqrt{39}$ = ± 0.0062
G) RSS High Alt., Subsonic	± 0.024	± 0.042 / $\sqrt{39}$ = ± 0.0066

Table D-7. 0–15 psid Delta Pressure Transducer Elemental Errors with Second-Order Curve Fits for Each Transducer

Error Source	Bias (psi)	Precision (2S, psi)
A) Calibration	N/A	N/A
B) Nonlinearity	N/A	N/A
C) Hysteresis/Precision	N/A	±0.045
D) Zero Shift	N/A	N/A
E) Sensitivity Shift ($\pm 0.0043\%R$ @ $\pm 10°F$)		
E1) Low Alt., Supersonic	N/A	±0.00035
E2) High Alt., Subsonic	N/A	±0.00013
F) RSS Low Alt., Supersonic	N/A	±0.045
G) RSS High Alt., Subsonic	N/A	±0.045

Table D-8. 0–50 psi High-Response Transducer Elemental Errors with Improved Temperature Control

	Uncertainty			
	Low Alt., Supersonic		High Alt., Subsonic	
Measured Pressure	psi	(%R)	psi	(%R)
Total pressure (ram)				
Baseline	±0.138	(±0.34%)	±0.126	(±5.3%)
5 psid range ΔP	±0.135	(±0.33%)	±0.126	(±5.3%)
Second-order fits (15 psid ΔP)	±0.138	(±0.34%)	±0.128	(±5.4%)
Dynamic distortion				
Baseline	±0.087	(±1.67%)	±0.087	(±13.1%)
5 psid range ΔP	±0.055	(±1.06%)	±0.056	(±8.1%)
Second-order fits (15 psid ΔP)	±0.087	(±1.67%)	±0.087	(±13.1%)
Better HR temp. control	±0.085	(±1.63%)	±0.087	(±13.1%)

Table D-9. Illustration of Uncertainty Improvements with Changes in Data Analysis, Selection, and Use

All of these changes are now summarized in Table D-9 so that the experimenter can decide upon which to do with the money and time available. Some are significant and worth the effort; others are not.

As can be seen in Table D-9, the only action that has any real effect is to go to second-order curve fits, and that improved only the dynamic distortion pressure measurements. It should be done, however, if the need for the accuracy improvement, reduced uncertainty, is there.

With the above gory details, it can be seen that uncertainty analysis can evaluate the potential impact of measurement system changes on the uncertainty before proceeding with the expensive task of implementing them.

Appendix H:
Alternate Measurement Uncertainty Analysis Approach

APPENDIX H

Alternate Measurement Uncertainty Analysis Approach

Harmonization With the International Standards Organization Publication: Guide to the Expression of Uncertainty in Measurement

Background:

Events subsequent to the first printing of this book have resulted in several new options for handling and presenting measurement uncertainty estimates. The International Standards Organization (ISO) **Guide to the Expression of Uncertainty in Measurement** (hereinafter referred to as the **Guide**) was published. There have been numerous written communications between the American Society of Mechanical Engineers (ASME) Performance Test Code (PTC) 19.1 Committee on Measurement Uncertainty charged with updating, the U. S. National Standard on measurement uncertainty, **PTC19.1, Measurement Uncertainty** (hereinafter referred to as **PTC19.1**), and the ISO, TAG4, WG3 authors of the **Guide**. Several meetings have occurred between the ISO **Guide** authors and the ASME committee, PTC19.1. These events have lead to agreement that has resulted in the harmonization of the principles of this text, **PTC19.1**, and the ISO **Guide**. These enhancements are likely to be included in the U. S. National Standard on Measurement Uncertainty. They may be used without violating the principles presented in this text, and, in many cases will result in a simpler measurement uncertainty model. This harmonized model is described in the following paragraphs.

The material presented here will include I) a simple U_{RSS} measurement uncertainty model for a result and for an average result, II) the proper handling of additional complications including small degrees of freedom, alternate confidence and uniform systematic uncertainty distributions, and, III) a calculation example.

I) A Simple U_{RSS} Measurement Uncertainty Model:

The principles of the ISO **Guide** and the **PTC19.1** are embodied in the simplified measurement uncertainty model, Equations H-1 and H-2.

For a result:

$$U_{95} = \pm(2)[(B/2)^2 + (S_{\bar{X}})^2]^{1/2} \tag{H-1}$$

This is actually a simplified U_{RSS} (U_{95}) where:

$B = \pm[\Sigma(b_i)^2]^{1/2}$
   It is the normally distributed systematic component of uncertainty 95% confidence.
b_i = The normally distributed systematic uncertainty source i, at 95% confidence.
$S_{\bar{X}} = \pm[\Sigma(S_{\bar{X}_i})^2]^{1/2}$
   The standard deviation of a result. It is the random component of uncertainty.

$S_{\overline{X}_i} = S_{X_i}/\sqrt{N_i}$

  The standard deviation of the average for random uncertainty source i.

$S_{Xi} = [\Sigma(X_i - \overline{X})^2/(n - 1)]^{1/2}$

  The standard deviation of random uncertainty source i with average $\overline{X}$ and number of data points n.

N_i = The number of values affected by uncertainty source i that are averaged.

(2) = Student's t for degrees of freedom ≥ 30.

For an average result:

If an experiment is run several times, say N times. The final result will be an average of the several runs. In that case the uncertainty is calculated by Equation H-2.

$$U_{95} = \pm(2)[(B/2)^2 + (S_{\overline{X}})^2/(N)]^{1/2} \qquad (H-2)$$

where N = The number of results averaged.

Type "A" and Type "B" Uncertainty Sources:

The ISO **Guide** recommends identifying uncertainty sources as either Type "A" for which there is data to calculate a standard deviation, or Type "B" for which there is not. If this identification is desired, subscripts of "A" or "B" may be added to the elemental uncertainty estimates, both systematic and random.

The ISO **Guide** does not address the grouping of uncertainty sources. Grouping them by their effect, systematic or random, is recommended. This approach is in agreement with the principles of this Text, PTC19.1 or the ISO **Guide**.

Degrees of Freedom:

Note that throughout this simple analysis, degrees of freedom are assumed to be ≥ 30 for all uncertainty sources, both systematic and random, and for the final uncertainty itself.

Comments:

Using the term (B/2) has the effect of including in the uncertainty Equations H-1 and H-2 an equivalent one standard deviation for the systematic uncertainty sources while also permitting their tabulation as 95% confidence estimates, their most likely appearance to experimenters. This also means that as long as one can assume that historical tabulations of systematic uncertainty source estimates are 95% confidence estimates for normal distributions, those tabulations and their associated uncertainty estimates need not be redone in order to be in conformance with the principles of the ISO **Guide**.

II) Additional Complications:

In the vast majority of cases, the new simple uncertainty model will be adequate. However, three major additonal complications are possible with the new, simple uncertainty model. One is the possibility of small (< 30) degrees of freedom. A second is the handling of other than 95% confidence. The third is working with other than normal distributions for estimates of systematic uncertainties.

1) Small degrees of freedom (< 30):

If the degrees of freedom associated with the elemental random uncertainties are < 30, it is necessary to use the Welch-Satterthwaite (W/S) approximation to determine the degrees of freedom for which Student's t may be selected to yield the U_{95} uncertainty. In that case, the (b_i) must also be included in the W/S calculation as $(b_i/2)$ and, in the absence of data sets, should be assumed to have infinite degrees of freedom.

2) Alternate (Other than) 95% Confidence Uncertainty Estimates:

If an uncertainty estimate of other than 95% confidence is desired, merely change the (2) multiplier in the front of Equations H-1 and H-2 to the appropriate Student's t for the degrees of freedom and confidence of interest. For degrees of freedom that are ≥ 30, use $t = 2.58$ for 99% confidence and $t = 3.00$ for 99.7% confidence.

3) The Assumption of Uniform Systematic Uncertainty Distributions:

If some of the elemental systematic uncertainty sources are thought not to be normal distributions but uniform (the only other realistic choice), the b_i are then estimated by Equation H-3.

$$b_i = \pm[2(L)/\sqrt{3}] \tag{H-3}$$

This is the elemental systematic uncertainty for error source i, estimated as two standard deviations for a uniform distribution.
L = The ± limits of the uniform distribution for systematic uncertainty source i.

Note that an equivalent one standard deviation for a uniform distribution with limits ±L is $L/\sqrt{3}$. The use of the multiplier (2) returns us to two standard deviations for each uniform systematic uncertainty source.

III) Example Calculation:

To see how this type of uncertainty calculation works, consider the data presented in Table 8-3 on page 164 and repeated here.

Error Source	Systematic Unc., or, ± Bias (b_i)	Random Unc., $S_{\bar{X}i}$, or, Precision Index (S)	Degrees of Frdm	Uncertainty ± U_{ADD}
Delta P	0.0013	0.00025	>30	0.0018
Air flow	0.0030	0.00175	>30	0.0065
Cooling air	0.0039	—	—	0.0039
Fuel flow	0.0011	0.00075	>30	0.0026
Burner P	0.0021	0.00105	>30	0.0043
RSS	0.0056	0.00219	>30	0.0100

(Remember that $U_{ADD} = \pm[B + t_{95}S]$.)

Table 8-3 Turbine Efficiency Elemental Errors in Result Units

If one were to adopt the ISA **Guide** format for Type "A" and Type "B" uncertainty sources, Table 8-3 might look like this:

Error Source	Systematic Unc., or, ± Bias (bi)	Random Unc., $S_{\bar{X}i}$, or, Precision Index (S)	Degrees of Frdm
Delta P	0.0013$_B$	0.00025	>30
Air flow	0.0030$_B$	0.00175$_A$	>30
Cooling air	0.0039$_B$	—	—
Fuel flow	0.0011$_A$	0.00075$_A$	>30
Burner P	0.0021$_B$	0.00105$_A$	>30
RSS	0.0056	0.00219	>30

Simplified Uncertainty Model:

The measurement uncertainty calculated by Equation H-1 would be:

$$U_{95} = (2)[(0.0056/2)^2 + (0.00219)^2]^{1/2}$$
$$= 0.00711 \qquad \text{(H-4)}$$

This is slightly smaller than the U_{ADD} (U_{99}) uncertainty of 0.0100 as expected since a smaller confidence should be a smaller uncertainty interval.

Small Degrees of Freedom:

Now suppose that the random uncertainties have small (<30) degrees of freedom. Table 8-3 might then look like this:

Error Source	Systematic Unc., or, ± Bias (b$_i$)	Degrees of Frdm	Random Unc., $S_{\bar{X}i}$, or, Precision Index (S)	Degrees of Frdm
Delta P	0.0013$_a$	∞	0.00025$_A$	10
Air flow	0.0030$_B$	∞	0.00175$_A$	6
Cooling air	0.0039$_B$	—	—	—
Fuel flow	0.0011$_A$	30	0.00075$_A$	9
Burner P	0.0021$_B$	∞	0.00105$_A$	3
RSS	0.0056	*	0.00219	*

Note that ∞ has been assumed as the degrees of freedom for a Type "B" systematic uncertainty, or bias, source because it is assumed that those values are well known.

*Use the Welch-Satterthwaite approximation, Equation H-5, as follows for the degrees of freedom associated with the uncertainty.

Table 8-3 Using Type "A" and Type "B" Uncertainty Sources and Small Degrees of Freedom (<30) Turbine Efficiency Elemental Errors in Result Units

$$\nu = \frac{[\Sigma(S_i)^2 + \Sigma(b_i/2)^2]^2}{\{\Sigma[(S_i)^4/\nu_i + (b_i/2)^4/\nu_i]\}} \qquad \text{(H-5)}$$

(Remember it is necessary to use the (b$_i$/2) as estimates of one standard deviation for the systematic uncertainties used in Equation H-5.)

$$= \frac{[4.7900*10^{-6} + 7.8750*10^{-6}]^2}{[2.0039*10^{-12} + 0.30502*10^{-14}]}$$
$$= 79.9 \sim 79 \text{ degrees of freedom.}$$

This means that we are over 30 degrees of freedom for U_{95}; use Student's t equal to 2.00. Therefore, our uncertainty interval has not changed from Equation H-4.

If in the very unlikely event that the degrees of freedom for any of the b_i terms drops below 30, all b_i must be listed as their equivalent one standard deviation. Then they are RSS'd and then doubled before being used in Equations H-1 or H-2. Degrees of freedom would still be handled by the Welch-Satterthwaite approximation, Equation H-5 with the b_i doubled as in Equations H-1 and H-2.

The Presence of Some Uniform Systematic Uncertainty Distributions:

Suppose some the estimates of elemental systematic uncertainties were from uniform rather than the previously assumed normal distributions. Table 8-3 might look like this:

| Error Source | Systematic | | Degrees of Frdm | Random | Degrees of Frdm |
	$\pm$ Bias Limit (L_i)	Unc., or, $\pm$ Bias* (b_i)		Unc., $S_{\bar{X}i}$, or, Precision Index (S)	
Delta P	0.0013_B	0.0015_B	∞	0.00025_A	10
Air flow	0.0030_B	0.0035_B	∞	0.00175_A	6
Cooling air	0.0039_B	0.0045_B	—	—	—
Fuel flow	—	0.0011_A**	30	0.00075_A	9
Burner P	0.0021_B	0.0024_B	∞	0.00105_A	3
RSS	—	0.0065	***	0.00219	***

*Note that the previous Bias estimates have been used as the Bias Limits here (or systematic uncertainty limits for uniform distributions). The conversion to Bias, or systematic uncertainty for each elemental error source was accomplished by Equation H-3.

**This term is $2S_{\bar{x}}$ from data and is a 95% confidence for a normal distribution.

***Again, degrees of freedom are obtained with the Welch-Satterthwaite approximation which will yield a degrees of freedom well over 30 so we can use Student's t = 2.00 for U_{95}.

Table 8-3 Using Type "A" and Type "B" Uncertainty Sources and Small Degrees of Freedom and with some Uniform Bias Distributions Turbine Efficiency Elemental Errors in Result Units

$$b_i = \pm[2(L)/\sqrt{3}] \tag{H-3}$$

The U_{95} measurement uncertainty is then calculated as follows:

$$\begin{aligned} U_{95} &= \pm(2)[(B/2)^2 + ((S_{\bar{X}})^2)]^{1/2} \\ &= \pm(2)[(0.0065/2)^2 + (0.00219)^2]^{1/2} \\ &= \pm0.0078 \end{aligned}$$

Conclusion:

It is interesting to note how little difference there is in these uncertainty estimates. However, those differences are evidence of the slightly different uncertainty models and need to be expressed as shown to be in accordance with the ISO **Guide.** That model is really a type of U_{RSS} also covered in the text.

Appendix I:
Solutions to All Exercises

APPENDIX I

Solutions to All Exercises

Unit 2

Exercise 2-1. *Student t*

    a. $S_{\bar{x}} = S_X/(N)^{1/2}$

    b. Prec. $= t_{95}S_{\bar{X}} = t_{95}S_X/(N)^{1/2}$

    c. 95% of the time, μ will be contained in the interval $(\bar{X} - t_{95}S_X/(N)^{1/2})$
       $\leq \mu \leq (\bar{X} + t_{95}S_X/(N)^{1/2})$

    d. 1. Prec. Ave. $= t_{95}S_X/(N)^{1/2} = 3.74/(12)^{1/2} = 1.08$
         2. see (c).

Exercise 2-2. *Pooling*

    a. 301 (most data)

    b. $2.131 * 325/(16)^{1/2} = 173$ $3.182 * 280/(4)^{1/2} = 445$
       $2.179 * 297/(13)^{1/2} = 179$ $2.365 * 291/(8)^{1/2} = 243$
       $2.074 * 301/(23)^{1/2} = 130$
       (Remember $N = \nu + 1$)

    c. 304; 59

Exercise 2-3. *Dependent Calibration*

    a. Separate calibration (in the same calibration facility) will reduce the calibration precision error by averaging but will cost more. An uncertainty analysis and a cost analysis are needed to determine the cost effectiveness. With the high cost of gasoline, extraordinary measures are being taken to improve the accuracy of measuring flow.

    b. A student once said, "It depends upon whether or not my cousin owns the independent calibration laboratory." However, the right answer is: Independent calibrations (different labs) would reduce both calibration bias and precision error. An uncertainty analysis and a cost analysis are needed.

    c. This will produce "linkage" or dependency in the two flows.

    d. In the general case, there are many different input and output flows. A weighted average based on the precision (variances) of the flow rates is often employed. Least squares regression is used to establish the weighting factors. Some writers have suggested weighting by uncertainties rather than by precision error only. This is described in Unit 6.

Unit 3

Exercise 3-1. *Bias Limit*

    a. $B = (\Sigma B_i^2)^{1/2} = 10.68$

    b. 19.47

Exercise 3-2. *Precision Index*

    a. $S = (1^2 + 2^2)^{1/2} = 2.24\%$

b.
$$\nu = \frac{(1^2 + 2^2)^2}{\dfrac{1^4}{10} + \dfrac{2^4}{20}} = \frac{25}{\dfrac{2 + 16}{20}} = 27.8$$

(Truncate for conservative answer)
$\nu = 27$

c. $t_{95,27} = 2.052$ (Note: the subscript 27 is for the degrees of freedom)
$$t_{95} * S = 2.052 * 2.24\% = 4.60\%$$

If the bias error is zero or negligible, about 95% of the time the true value should lie within the interval of the average plus or minus $t_{95} S_{\bar{x}}$

Exercise 3-3. *Combining Degrees of Freedom Problem*

Just sum over i to obtain, for j = 1,
$$S_1 = [\Sigma (S_{i1})^2]^{1/2}.$$
Proceed similarly for j = 2, 3, or . . . number of categories.

Exercise 3-4. *Truncating Degrees of Freedom Problem*

Truncating yields a lesser degrees of freedom with an associated larger t_{95}. This results in a slightly larger random error component of the uncertainty and slightly larger uncertainty. Thus, this overestimating of uncertainty is a safer path for decisions, thus, more conservative.

Exercise 3-5. *Root-Sum-Square Uncertainty Interval*

$$U_{RSS}^- = -[(B^-)^2 + (-t_{95}S)^2]^{1/2} = -0.74$$
$$U_{RSS}^+ = +[(B^+)^2 + (+t_{95}S)^2]^{1/2} = +0.40$$

Exercise 3-6. *Scale and Truth*

a.   Consideration

b.   Truth in this case is the reading on the doctor's scale.

c.–e. Consideration

Unit 4

Exercise 4-1. *Terminology*

a. ϵ is the real, true random error in any one measurement.
$2S_X/\sqrt{N}$ is the random error component of the uncertainty for large degrees of freedom, > 30. The distribution of error it represents is caused by the true error, ϵ, in each measurement.

b. β is the true bias error for any one measurement or group of measurements in a process.
B is the bias limit; it is the estimate of the true bias error, β.

c. δ is the true total error in one measurement. It is $(\epsilon + \beta)$.
U is the measurement uncertainty usually noted as either U_{ADD} or U_{RSS}. It is the estimate of the total error or uncertainty.

Exercise 4-2. *Pooling Review*

a. The s values represent three estimates of the population standard deviation, σ.

b. 50.0; it is the s with the most data.

c. 43.0

d. 34

Exercise 4-3. *Delta*

a. 1.72 and 1.51, respectively.

b. No, they also include process variations.

c. −0.9, −1.0, and −0.6

d. 0.21

e. $0.21/\sqrt{2} = 0.15$

f. Two measurement systems can be used to evaluate the precision of either if they are measuring the same process. Using only one would yield a precision error larger than that caused by the measurement.

Exercise 4-4. *Interfacility Results*

a. The best estimate available for the orifice flow.

b. $\pm t_{95}S_X = \pm(2.447 \times 0.2) = \pm0.5$ lbs/sec

c. (b) represents the scatter between laboratories. The closeness of the 12.0 lbs/sec to the true value is obtained by dividing (b) by $\sqrt{7}$, yielding 0.18 lbs/sec. That is, 12 ± 0.18 lbs/sec contains the true value 95% of the time.

d. Each laboratory may interpret (b) above as the bias between laboratories or the bias limit to assign to each one.

Exercise 4-5. *Bias Impact*

a. 66

b. No. It assumes all the elemental error components work to their limits in the same direction at the same time. That is not realistic.

c. 60.2

d. No. Same as b above for the largest, most influential elemental errors.

e. 37.6

f. Yes. All elemental error components have the chance to cancel and this calculation considers that.

g. e

Exercise 4-6. *Back-to-Back Calibration*

a. $U_{CAL} = [B_{CAL}^2 + (t_{95}S_{CAL})^2]^{1/2}$ (fossilized)

$= \{[1/(2)^{1/2}]^2 + [2/(2)^{1/2}]^2\}^{1/2} = (5/2)^{1/2}$ (all bias)

b. $B_{CAL} = [1/(2)^{1/2}]\%$, $S_{CAL} = [1/(2)^{1/2}]\%$

c. No calibration error!

d. Correct for documented drift in time. This would increase the above errors by the error in designating the drift in time.

Exercise 4-7. *Observable Bias Error*

a. Unknown. The $\pm0.5\%$ is only the precision error or random error component of the uncertainty. The bias limit is unknown, so the uncertainty is unknown.

b. No. A consistent shift of all the data cannot be observed; only the scatter in the data can be observed.

c. It could be large but can't be calculated. The uncertainty is unknown. If the bias limit is large, there is great risk attendant to any decision based on these test results.

Exercise 4-8. *Compressor Uncertainty*

a. There is a great risk in misinterpreting the test results. The test should be postponed until the uncertainty can be improved. Review the uncertainty analysis to determine:
   1. bias or precision problems and
   2. which measurand is involved (or are there several?).
   From these answers, analyze the alternatives to select the most cost-effective improvement.

b. A simple view would be $\pm 2S = \pm 1.2\%$, i.e., close enough!

c. (1) Take more data points and average, or (2) use more redundant instrumentation for the most imprecise measurand, or (3) obtain a more precise measuring probe, transducer, or instrument.

d. 1. Better calibration method or standard.
   2. More accurate instrumentation.
   3. Independent calibration of redundant instruments.
   4. Concomitant variable.

Unit 5

Exercise 5-1.

Error propagation is needed to combine errors from several sources and evaluate their effects on the test or experimental result. It is not possible to combine errors in temperature and pressure, for example, into their impact on flow until the temperature and pressure errors are converted into the result units of flow. This is what error propagation does.

Exercise 5-2. *Orifice Problem*

a. $S_{P_{up}} = 2.8835$; $S_{P_{dn}} = 2.9925$

b. 1) $S_{\Delta P_i} = [(1)^2(S_{P_{up}})^2 + (-1)^2(S_{P_{dn}})^2]^{1/2}$
   2) $S_{\Delta P_i} = [(2.8835)^2 + (2.9925)^2]^{1/2} = 4.1557$
   3) $S_{\Delta P_i} = [(1)^2(S_{P_{up}})^2 + (-1)^2(S_{P_{dn}})^2 + 2(1)(-1)\rho(S_{P_{up}})(S_{P_{dn}})]^{1/2}$
   4) Use Formula in 3). Remember $\rho = 0.9983$.
      $S_{\Delta P_d} = [(2.8835)^2 + (2.9925)^2$
      $\qquad -2(.9983)(2.8835)(2.9925)]^{1/2} = 0.203$
   5) Just list the differences between each upstream and its corresponding downstream pressure.
   6) $S_{\Delta P} = 0.201$
   7) The correct $S_{\Delta P}$ is answer 6. There the actual delta pressure data has been used to calculate the standard deviation of those deltas. However, answer 4 is also correct as the error propagation has properly considered the dependency, or lack of independence, of the delta pressure measurements. Answer 6 and 4 agree as proof of the Taylor's Series error propagation method. Answer 2 is dead wrong. Included in its calculation of the standard deviation of the delta pressures is the standard deviation of some effect that is shifting both the upstream and downstream pressure measurements. Those measurements are correlated and can't be assumed to be independent as is done in the usual Taylor's Series error propagation. The lesson? Watch out for nonindependent error sources. You can get killed!

Exercise 5-3. *Word Problem*

When air flow is contained explicitly in both gross thrust and drag equations, it is not correct to first propagate the errors in air flow into error in net thrust and then follow (by propagation) the errors in air flow into drag, finishing by propagating the errors in gross thrust and drag into net thrust. In that case, the errors in air flow are linked to the error propagation results obtained for both gross thrust and drag. Air flow error is implicit in the propagation of gross thrust and drag errors into the final result of net thrust. This will not properly account for the correlation that then results. What is necessary is to propagate the error in air flow, gross thrust, and drag in one expression through to net thrust. In that case the linked error of air flow will be explicitly present in the net thrust equation and properly handled by the Taylor's Series error propagation.

Exercise 5-4.

The Welch-Satterthwaite equation for combining degrees of freedom is given as Eq. (3-6) for this simple, all-the-same-error category, exercise.

$$\nu = [\Sigma (S_j)^2]^2 / \{\Sigma [(S_j)^4 / \nu_j]\}$$

For the $S_{\bar{x}}$ data in Table 5-2, Eq. (3-6) becomes:

$$\nu = \frac{[(0.20)^2 + (0.20)^2 + (0.02)^2 + (0.50)^2]^2}{[(0.20)^4/45 + (0.20)^4/8 + (0.02)^4/3 + (0.50)^4/20]}$$

$$= (0.109164)/(0.003361) = 32.48$$

$$\cong 32 \text{ (always round down)}$$

For the $S_{\bar{x}}$ data in Table 5-3, Eq. (3-6) becomes:

$$\nu = \frac{[(0.57)^2 + (0.30)^2 + (0.20)^2]^2}{[(0.57)^4/32 + (0.30)^4/16 + (0.20)^4/1]}$$

$$= (0.206934)/(0.005405) = 38.29$$

$$\cong 38 \text{ (always round down)}$$

Exercise 5-5.

Assuming equal flow in each of the meters, the equation for the total flow, F, is

$$F = A + B + C$$

where A, B, and C are the flows in each of the three meters. Using Eq. (5-16), the following error propagation equation is obtained for bias error. Simply substituting S for B in this equation will yield the error propagation equation for precision error.

$$B_F = [(\partial F/\partial A)^2 (B_A)^2 + (\partial F/\partial B)^2 (B_B)^2 + (\partial F/\partial C)^2 (B_C)^2$$

$$+ 2(\partial F/\partial A)(\partial F/\partial B)\rho_{AB}(B_A)(B_B)$$

$$+ 2(\partial F/\partial C)(\partial F/\partial B)\rho_{CB}(B_C)(B_B)$$

$$+ 2(\partial F/\partial A)(\partial F/\partial C)\rho_{AC}(B_A)(B_C)]^{1/2}$$

This is the error propagation equation for absolute units. It will also work for relative units, % terms, but the sensitivities or influence coefficients will be more complicated.

Exercise 5-6. *Decision Time*

a. For all independent errors, all the correlation coefficients in the error propagation equation, ρ, are 0.0 and the three cross-product terms go to zero. The numerical values of the partial derivative terms, the influ-ence coefficients, or sensitivities are all 1.0 by inspection. If all the bias errors and precision errors are 1.0 gal/min, the test, or experimental bias and precision index, is calculated as follows:

$$B = [(1.0)^2(1.0)^2 + (1.0)^2(1.0)^2 + (1.0)^2(1.0)^2]^{1/2}$$
$$= (3.0)^{1/2} = 1.7 \text{ gal/min}$$
$$S = [(1.0)^2(1.0)^2 + (1.0)^2(1.0)^2 + (1.0)^2(1.0)^2]^{1/2}$$
$$= (3.0)^{1/2} = 1.7 \text{ gal/min}$$

Eq. (5.21) is the error propagation equation for three meters in series. By inspection and comparison to the above, it is seen that for the series case the bias is 1/3 the above, as is the precision index. Therefore, for independent errors (including bias) the series network is more accu-rate.

b. For the case in which the bias errors are completely dependent, the correlation coefficients, ρ, in the above general error propagation equa-tion are 1.0. The following is then obtained for bias error:

$$B = [(1.0)^2(1.0)^2 + (1.0)^2(1.0)^2 + (1.0)^2(1.0)^2$$
$$+ 2(1.0)(1.0)(1.0)(1.0)(1.0)$$
$$+ 2(1.0)(1.0)(1.0)(1.0)(1.0)$$
$$+ 2(1.0)(1.0)(1.0)(1.0)(1.0)]^{1/2}$$
$$= 3.0$$

The same answer is obtained for precision as obtained above, that is, S = 1.7, since precision errors from one time to another cannot ever be dependent.

For the series case, the bias error is, by inspection,

$$B = 3.0/3.0 = 1.0.$$

The series case is still more accurate, and correlated bias has increased the total bias. This does not always happen, but the Taylor's Series approach will give the correct answer for every circumstance.

Unit 6

Exercise 6-1. *Why Weight Problem*

a. A weighted result will be more accurate (lower uncertainty) than any of the methods being weighted.

b. All weighting formulae must have the same units for all the error terms. That is, all bias terms, all precision terms, and all uncertainty terms must have the same units, usually those of the test result.

Exercise 6-2. *Weighting by Uncertainty*

a.
$$\underline{\underline{x}} = \frac{\Sigma N_i \bar{x}_i}{\Sigma N_i} = 97.7$$

b.
$$W_2 = \frac{(U_1 U_3)^2}{W_T} \quad \{W_T = [(U_1 U_2)^2 + (U_2 U_3)^2 + (U_3 U_1)^2]\}$$

$$W_3 = \frac{(U_1 U_2)^2}{W_T}$$

c.
$$W_1 = \frac{48841}{48841 + 18496 + 10816} = 0.62494$$

$W_2 = 0.23666$

$W_3 = 0.13840$

Check: $W_1 + W_2 + W_3 = 1$ if correct.

d. $\underline{\underline{X}} = 95.83$; $\underline{\underline{U}}_{ADD} = \underline{\underline{B}} + t\underline{\underline{S}}_{\bar{x}}$

$\underline{\underline{B}} = [(0.62494 * 6)^2 + (0.23666 * 10)^2 + (0.13840 * 8)^2]^{1/2} = 4.57$

$2\underline{\underline{S}}_{\bar{x}} = [(0.62494 * 2)^2 + (0.23666 * 3)^2 + (0.13840 * 9)^2]^{1/2} = 1.9$

$\underline{\underline{U}}_{ADD} = 4.57 + 1.9 = 6.47$

$\underline{\underline{U}}_{RSS} = [(4.57)^2 + (1.9)^2]^{1/2} = 4.95$

e. Weighting produces a more accurate average, smaller uncertainty.

Unit 7

Exercise 7-1. *Outliers: Thompson's Tau* (τ)

a. 1. $\bar{X} = 14.158$ $S = 120.7$ $N = 19$
    2. 334 is suspect outlier.
    3. $\delta = |334 - 14.158| = 319.842$
    4. $\tau = 1.881$
    5. $\tau S = 1.881 * 120.7 = 227.0$
    6. $\delta > \tau S$ [319.842 > 227.0]. Therefore, 334 is an outlier.

b. 1. $\bar{X} = -3.611$ $S = 95.3$ $N = 18$
    2. -220 is suspect outlier.
    3. $\delta = |-220 - (-3.611)| = 216.389$
    4. $\tau = 1.876$
    5. $\tau S = 1.876 * 95.3 = 178.8$
    6. $\delta > \tau S = (216.4 > 178.8)$. Therefore, -220 is an outlier.

c. 1. $\bar{X} = 9.118$ $S = 80.9$ $N = 17$
    2. 166 is suspect outlier.
    3. $\delta = |166 - 9.118| = 156.882$
    4. $\tau = 1.871$
    5. $\tau S = 1.871 * 80.9 = 151.4$
    6. $\delta > \tau S$ (156.882 > 151.4). Therefore, 166 is an outlier.

d. 1. $\bar{X} = -0.688$ $S = 72.4$ $N = 16$
    2. 129 is suspect outlier.
    3. $\delta = |129 - (-0.688)| = 129.688$
    4. $\tau = 1.865$
    5. $\tau S = 1.865 * 72.4 = 135.026$
    6. $\delta < \tau S$ (129.688 < 135.026). Therefore, 129 is *not* an outlier!

Exercise 7-2. *Curve Fitting*

a. For CO_2-A, Order 3
   For CO_2-B, Order 5

b. No, there may not be enough data for these third- or fifth-order fits.

c. All CO_2-A ranges: $0.028 \approx 0.044$ (0–5%) and $0.020 \approx 0.022$ (0–2%); close enough.
   Two CO_2-B ranges: $0.101 \approx 0.115$ (0–18%) and $0.035 \approx 0.044$ (0–5%); close enough.
   The 2SEE scatter in the above approximates the standard calibration gas error.

Exercise 7-3. *Least-Squares Curve Fit*

$$\Delta = y - Ax^2 - Bx$$

$$\Delta^2 = y^2 - 2Ayx^2 - 2Byx + A^2x^4 + 2ABx^3 + B^2x^2$$

$$\Sigma\Delta^2 = \Sigma y^2 - 2A\Sigma yx^2 - 2B\Sigma yx + A^2\Sigma x^4 + 2AB\Sigma x^3 + B^2\Sigma x^2$$

Minimize $\Sigma\Delta^2$ with respect to A and B:

$$\frac{\partial(\Sigma\Delta^2)}{\partial A} = -2\Sigma yx^2 + 2A\Sigma x^4 + 2B\Sigma x^3 = 0$$

$$\frac{\partial(\Sigma\Delta^2)}{\partial B} = -2\Sigma yx + 2A\Sigma x^3 + 2B\Sigma x^2 = 0$$

Solve for A and B:

$$A = \frac{\Sigma x^2 \Sigma yx^2 - \Sigma yx \Sigma x^3}{\Sigma x^2 \Sigma x^4 - (\Sigma x^3)^2}$$

$$B = \frac{\Sigma yx - A\Sigma x^3}{\Sigma x^2}$$

Exercise 7-4. *Correlation*

a. At 95% $+1.00 > \rho_A > +0.97$
             $+0.94 > \rho_B > +0.40$
             $-0.04 > \rho_C > -0.87$

b. At 99% $+1.00 > \rho_A > +0.92$
             $+0.95 > \rho_B > +0.18$
             $+0.17 > \rho_C > -0.92$

c. At 95%   All significant
   At 99% r_A and r_B are significant

d. This is simple X vs. Y plots.

e. Two outliers in data set B; eliminate them.

f. $r_B = -0.009$; not significant.

g. Even high correlation coefficients (close to ± 1.0) are not always significant.

Exercise 7-5. *Probability Plot*

a. Just line up the ordered data points with the ordered median ranks.

b. Plots

c.

Data Set	Line	Conclusion	$\overline{X}$	S_X	Outliers?
A	Str.	Normal Data	≈ -0.65	≈ 1.18	No
B	Str.	Normal Data	≈ 0.17	≈ 0.61	One
C	Two	Bimodal	—	—	No

d.

Data Set	Calculated	
	$\overline{X}$	S
A	-0.647	1.123
B	0.064	0.797
C	1.792	2.204

e. Rework data set B after outlier is removed. Determine source of bimodality in data set C.

Index

INDEX